LANGUAGE ARTS 200

Teacher's Guide

Author:
Pam Slagter, B.A.

Managing Editor:
Alan Christopherson, M.S.

Editor:
Jennifer Davis, B.S.

Alpha Omega
PUBLICATIONS

804 N. 2nd Ave. E.
Rock Rapids, IA 51246-1759

LANGUAGE ARTS 200

LIFEPAC® Overview

LANGUAGE ARTS SCOPE & SEQUENCE

KINDERGARTEN

Lessons 1-40	Lessons 41-80	Lessons 81-120	Lessons 121-160
Alphabet -say the alphabet **Colors** -recognize colors **Directions** -left to right **Following directions** -oral and written **Grammar** -form simple sentences **Listening skills** **Personal recognition** -read and write first name -know age and address -recognize names of family members **Phonics** -short *a, e, i* vowels -initial: *b, t, m, r, s, n, d, p, l* -form and read simple words -form rhyming words **Shapes** -circle, square, triangle, and rectangle -recognize shapes in objects **Stories and poems** -create simple stories and poems **Writing** -form circle and lines -*Aa, Bb, Dd, Ee, Ii, Ll, Mm, Nn, Pp, Rr, Ss,* and *Tt*	**Grammar** -sentences begin with capital, end with period **Patterns** -simple shape, color patterns **Personal recognition** -read and write first and last name **Phonics** -short *a, e, i, o,* and *u* vowels -initial: *k, c, ck, f, h, g, j, v, w, y, z, qu,* and *x* -read simple sentences **Position/direction concepts** -in/out, in front of/behind, up/down, on/off, open/closed, over/under **Sequencing** -alphabetical order -simple story **Shapes** -oval **Size concepts** -big/little, large/small **Writing** -*Kk, Cc, Ff, Hh, Oo, Gg, Jj, Vv, Ww, Uu, Yy, Zz, Qq,* and *Xx*	**Phonics** -recognize the short vowel sounds -recognize all initial consonant sounds -recognize long *a, e, i, o,* and *u* sounds -silent *e* -initial consonant digraphs: *sh, ch,* both soft and hard *th* -final consonant sounds: *_b, _ck, _k, _l* **Word recognition** -color words, number words, and shape words **Writing** -name -complete alphabet, capital and small letters -all color words -number words: *one, two, three, four, five, six* -shape words: *circle, square, triangle*	**Phonics** -recognize the long vowel sounds -initial consonant digraphs: *wh,* review *ch, sh, th* -recognize all final consonant sounds **Stories and poems** -create, tell, and recite stories and poems **Word recognition** -position/direction words: *up/down, high/low, in/inside, out/outside, top/bottom* -number words: *seven, eight, nine, ten* -shape words: *rectangle, oval, star* **Writing** -number words: *seven, eight, nine, ten* -shape words: *rectangle, oval, star* -position/direction words: *up/down, high/low, in/inside, out/outside, top/bottom*

LANGUAGE ARTS SCOPE & SEQUENCE

	Grade 1	Grade 2	Grade 3
UNIT 1	ALPHABET AND SHORT VOWEL SOUNDS • Short vowel sounds • Consonants • Main ideas • Rhyming words	KNOW YOUR NOUNS • Review vowels & consonants • Beginning, middle, ending sounds • Singular & plural nouns • Common & proper nouns	OLD AND NEW SKILLS • Vowels • Consonants • Sentence phrases • Capital letters • Reading skills
UNIT 2	RHYMING WORDS, ADDING "ING" • Kinds of sentences • Cardinal & ordinal numbers • Suffixes • Plurals • Classifying	ACTION VERBS • Vowel digraphs • Action words – verbs • Following directions • The dictionary • ABC order	BUILDING WORDS AND SENTENCES • Vowels – long, short • Questions • ABC order • Capital letters
UNIT 3	CONSONANT DIGRAPHS, SOFT C AND G • Consonant digraphs • Compounds • Syllables • Possessives • Contractions • Soft c and g	SIMPLE SENTENCES • R-controlled vowels • Consonant blends • Using capital letters • Subjects & verbs in sentences	WORDS: GETTING TO THE ROOTS • Root words • Dictionary guide words • Synonyms • Antonyms • Capital letters
UNIT 4	VERBS, BLENDS, AND SILENT LETTERS • Paragraphs • Silent letters • Sequencing • Subject-verb agreement	TYPES OF SENTENCES • Consonant digraphs • Statement, question, exclamation sentences • Using capital letters • The library	WORDS: HOW TO USE THEM • Noun • Verb • Adjective • Adverb • Irregular vowels • Composition
UNIT 5	LONG VOWELS AND SYLLABLES • Long vowels • Homonyms • Poetry • Syllables • Possessives • Contractions • Plurals • Suffixes	USING PUNCTUATION • Diphthongs • Punctuation review • Using a comma • Rules for making words plural • Writing a biography • Contractions	SENTENCE: START TO FINISH • Main idea • Capital letters and punctuation • Paragraphs • Making words plural
UNIT 6	R-CONTROLLED VOWELS AND PLURALS • R-controlled vowels • Writing stories • Pronouns • Following directions	ADJECTIVES • Rhyming words • Biblical poetry • Adjectives in sentences • Synonyms, antonyms • Thesaurus • Comparative, superlative adjectives	ALL ABOUT BOOKS • Main idea • Books • Stories • Poems • Critical thinking
UNIT 7	VOWEL DIGRAPHS AND SENTENCES • Vowel digraphs • Letters - business, friendly, invitations • Syllables	POSSESSIVE NOUNS • Introduction to letter writing • Pronunciation key • Possessive nouns • Silent consonants • Homonyms	READING AND WRITING • For directions • Friendly letters • Pronouns • Fact • Fiction
UNIT 8	VOWEL DIGRAPHS AND POSSESSIVES • Vowel digraphs • Subject-verb agreement • Compounds • Contractions • Possessives • Pronouns	PRONOUNS • Author's intent & use of titles • Predicting content • Suffixes • Character, setting, & plot • Analogies • Writing in cursive	READING SKILLS • For sequence • For detail • Verbs - being, compound • Drama
UNIT 9	DIPHTHONGS AND CONTRACTIONS • Vowel digraphs • Titles • Main ideas • Sentences • Paragraphs • Proper nouns	VERB TYPES AND TENSES • Review action verbs • Dividing words into syllables • State of being verbs • Past & present verb tenses	MORE READING & WRITING • For information • Thank-you letters • Book reports • Reference books
UNIT 10	PHONICS AND GRAMMAR REVIEW • Letters and sounds • Contractions • Plurals • Possessives • Sentences • Stories	LOOKING BACK • Nouns & verbs • Word division • Consonant blends, digraphs • Prefixes, suffixes, root words • Possessives • Pronouns, adjectives	LOOKING BACK • Reading for comprehension • Sentence punctuation • Writing letters • Parts of Speech

LANGUAGE ARTS SCOPE & SEQUENCE

	Grade 4	Grade 5	Grade 6
UNIT 1	WRITTEN COMMUNICATION • Word derivations • Story sequence • Writing an outline • Writing a report	STORY MESSAGES • Main idea • Plot • Character • Settings • Dialogue • Diphthong • Digraph	READING FOR A PURPOSE • Critical thinking • Research data • Parables • Synonyms
UNIT 2	SOUNDS TO WORDS • Hard and soft – c and g • Parts of dictionary • Accented syllables • Haiku Poetry	MAIN IDEAS • Poetry • Story • Synonyms • Compounds • Topic sentence • Adjectives • Nouns	FORMING NEW WORDS • Prefixes • Suffixes • Synonyms • Antonyms • Adjectives • Adverbs • Critical thinking
UNIT 3	WORDS: HOW TO USE THEM • Prefixes • Suffixes • Homonyms • Antonyms • Poetry • Stories • Writing an outline	WORDS TO STORIES • Subject • Predicate • Adverbs • Idioms • Critical thinking • Writing a short story	BETTER READING • Story elements • Author's purpose • Information sources • Outline
UNIT 4	MORE WORDS: HOW TO USE THEM • Parts of speech • Possession • Written directions • Verb tenses	WRITTEN REPORT • Outline • Four types of sentences • Metaphor • Simile • Writing the report	SENTENCES • Capitals • Punctuation • Four types of sentences • Author's purpose • Propaganda
UNIT 5	WRITING FOR CLARITY • Figures of speech • Capital letters • Punctuation marks • Writing stories	STORY ELEMENTS • Legend • Implied meaning • Dialogue • Quotations • Word order • Usage • Story elements	READING SKILLS • Following directions • Literary forms • Phrases • Nouns • Verbs • Paragraph structure
UNIT 6	FUN WITH FICTION • Book reports • Fiction • Nonfiction • Parables • Fables • Poetry	POETRY • Rhythm • Stanza • Symbolism • Personification • Irregular plurals	POETRY • Similes • Metaphors • Alliteration • Homonyms • Palindromes • Acronyms • Figures of speech
UNIT 7	FACT AND FICTION • Nouns • Verbs, • Contractions • Biography • Fables • Tall Tales	WORD USAGE • Nouns - common, plural, possessive • Fact • Opinion • Story • Main idea	STORIES • Story elements • Nouns • Pronouns • Vowel digraphs • Business letter
UNIT 8	GRAMMAR AND WRITING • Adjectives to compare • Adverbs • Figurative language • Paragraphs	ALL ABOUT VERBS • Tense • Action • Participles • Of being • Regular • Irregular • Singular • Plural	ANALYZING THE NEWS • Propaganda • News stories • Verbs - auxiliary, tenses • Adverbs
UNIT 9	THE WRITTEN REPORT • Planning a report • Finding information • Outline • Writing a report	READING FLUENCY • Speed reading • Graphic aids • Study skills • Literary forms	READING THE BIBLE • Parables • Proverbs • Hebrew - poetry, prophecy • Bible history • Old Testament law
UNIT 10	LOOKING BACK • Reading skills • Nouns • Adverbs • Written communication • Literary forms	LOOKING BACK • Literary forms • Parts of speech • Writing skills • Study skills	LOOKING BACK • Literary forms • Writing letters • Parts of speech • Punctuation

LANGUAGE ARTS SCOPE & SEQUENCE

	Grade 7	Grade 8	Grade 9
UNIT 1	WORD USAGE • Nouns - proper, common • Pronouns • Prefixes - Suffixes • Synonyms - Antonyms	IMPROVE COMMUNICATION • Roots • Inflections • Affixes • Interjections • Directions – oral, written • Non-verbal communication	STRUCTURE OF LANGUAGE • Nouns • Adjectives • Prepositions • Verbs • Adverbs • Conjunctions • Sentence parts • Diagram sentences
UNIT 2	MORE WORD USAGES • Speech – stress, pitch • Verbs – tenses • Principle parts • Story telling	ALL ABOUT ENGLISH • Origin of language • Classification–nouns, pronouns, verbs, adjectives, adverbs	NATURE OF LANGUAGE • Origin of language • Use – oral and written • Dictionary • Writing a paper
UNIT 3	BIOGRAPHIES • Biography as a form • Flashback technique • Deductive reasoning • Words – base, root	PUNCTUATION AND WRITING • Connecting and interrupting • The Essay • Thesis Statement	PRACTICAL ENGLISH • Dictionary use • Mnemonics • Writing a paper • Five-minute speech
UNIT 4	LANGUAGE STRUCTURE • Verbs – tenses • Principle parts • Sentence creativity • Speech – pitch, accent	WORDS • HOW TO USE THEM • Dictionary • Thesaurus • Accents • Diacritical marks • Standard • Nonstandard	SHORT STORY FUNDAMENTALS • Plot • Setting • Characterization • Conflict • Symbolism
UNIT 5	NATURE OF ENGLISH • Formal • Informal • Redundant expressions • Verb tenses • Subject–verb agreement	CORRECT LANGUAGE • Using good form • Synonyms • Antonyms • Homonyms • Good speaking qualities	LANGUAGE IN LITERATURE • Collective Nouns • Verbs • Use of comparisons • Gerunds • Participles • Literary genres
UNIT 6	MECHANICS OF ENGLISH • Punctuation • Complements • Modifiers • Clauses – subordinate, coordinate	LANGUAGE AND LITERATURE • History of English • Coordination and Subordination • Autobiography	MEANING IN POETRY AND PROSE • Reading for purpose • Reading for meaning • Reading persuasion • Understanding poetry
UNIT 7	THE HIDING PLACE: A STUDY GUIDE • Sequence of Events • Facts about characters • Author's purpose • Character sketch	CRITICAL THINKING • Word evaluation • The Paragraph – structure, coherence, introductory, concluding	COMMUNICATION • Planning a speech • Listening comprehension • Letters – business, informal, social
UNIT 8	LITERATURE • Nonfiction • Listening skills • Commas • Semicolons • Nonverbal communication	WRITE • LISTEN • READ • Business letters • Personal letters • Four steps to listen • Nonfiction	LIBRARY AND DRAMA • Library resources • Drama – history, elements, reading • *The Miracle Worker*
UNIT 9	COMPOSITIONS • Sentence types • Quality of paragraph • Pronunciation • Nonsense literature	SPEAK AND WRITE • Etymology • Modifiers • Person • Number • Tense • Oral report	STUDIES IN THE NOVEL • History • Define • Write • Critical essay • *Twenty Thousand Leagues Under the Sea*
UNIT 10	LOOKING BACK • Parts of speech • Sentence structure • Punctuation • How to communicate	LANGUAGE ELEMENTS IN REVIEW • Composition structure • Parts of speech • Critical thinking • Literary forms	LOOKING BACK • Communication – writing, speaking, listening • Using resources • Literature review • Diagram sentences

LANGUAGE ARTS SCOPE & SEQUENCE

	Grade 10	Grade 11	Grade 12
UNIT 1	THE DEVELOPMENT OF ENGLISH • Historical development • Varieties of English • Substandard & standard • Changes in English	STANDARD ENGLISH • Need for standard English • Guardians of the standard • Dictionaries • Types of standard English texts	THE WORTH OF WORDS • Word categories • Expository writing • Sentence structure • Diction
UNIT 2	LISTENING AND SPEAKING • Noun plurals • Suffixes • Creating a speech • Nature of listening	WRITING EFFECTIVE SENTENCES • Subordinate – clauses, conjunctions • Relative pronouns • Verbals • Appositives	STRUCTURE OF LANGUAGE • Parts of speech • Sentence Structure • Subordinate Phrases • Subordinate Clauses
UNIT 3	WRITING EFFECTIVE SENTENCES • Verbals • Phrases – prepositional, verbal • Sentence types • Diagram sentences	CLEAR CONNECTIONS: A WRITING WORKSHOP • Understanding pronouns • Using pronouns correctly • Using modifiers correctly • Parallel sentence structures	READ, RESEARCH, AND LISTEN • Reading skills • Resources for research • Taking Notes • Drawing Conclusions
UNIT 4	POWER OF WORDS • Etymology • Connotations • Poetic devices • Poetry – literal, figurative, symbolic	WHY STUDY READING? • Greek and Latin roots • Diacritical markings • Finding the main idea • Analyzing a textbook	GIFT OF LANGUAGE • Biblical origin • Koine Greek • Purpose of Grammar • Semantics
UNIT 5	ELEMENTS OF COMPOSITION • Paragraphs • Connectives • Transitions • Expository writing - elements, ideas	POETRY • Metrical feet • Sets • Musical effects • Universality • Imagery • Connotation	ENGLISH LITERATURE • Early England • Medieval England • Fourteenth century • Chaucer
UNIT 6	STRUCTURE AND READING • Subordinate clauses • Pronouns – gender, case, agreement • Reading for recognition	NONFICTION • Elements • Types – essays, diaries, newspaper, biography • Composition	ELIZABETHAN LITERATURE • Poetry • Prose • Drama • Essay
UNIT 7	ORAL READING AND DRAMA • Skills of oral reading • Drama – history, irony, elements, allegory • *Everyman*	AMERICAN DRAMA • Development • History • Structure • Purpose • *Our Town*	17TH AND 18TH CENTURY LITERATURE • Historical background • Puritan Literature • Common sense – satire • Sensibility
UNIT 8	THE SHORT STORY • Elements • Enjoying • Writing • The Literary Critique	STUDIES IN THE AMERICAN NOVEL • Eighteenth, nineteenth, twentieth Century • *The Old Man and the Sea* • The Critical Essay	CREATIVE WRITING • Fundamentals • Inspiration • Technique and style • Form and process
UNIT 9	THE NOVEL • Elements • *In His Steps* • The Critical Essay • The Book Review	RESEARCH • Stating the thesis • Research • Outline • Writing the paper	ROMANTIC AND VICTORIAN POETRY • Wordsworth • Coleridge • Gordon • Byron • Shelley • Keats • Tennyson • Hopkins • Robert and Elizabeth B. Browning
UNIT 10	LOOKING BACK • Writing skills • Speech skills • Poetry • Drama • Short stories • Novel	REVIEWING COMMUNICATION SKILLS AND LITERATURE • Analyzing written word • Effective sentences • Expository prose • Genres of American literature	LANGUAGE AND ENGLISH LITERATURE REVIEW • Creative writing • English literature – Medieval to Victorian

STRUCTURE OF THE LIFEPAC CURRICULUM

The LIFEPAC curriculum is conveniently structured to provide one Teacher's Guide containing teacher support material with answer keys and ten student worktexts for each subject at grade levels 2 through 12. The worktext format of the LIFEPACs allows the student to read the textual information and complete workbook activities all in the same booklet. The easy-to-follow LIFEPAC numbering system lists the grade as the first number(s) and the last two digits as the number of the series. For example, the Language Arts LIFEPAC at the 6th grade level, 5th book in the series would be LAN0605.

Each LIFEPAC is divided into three to five sections and begins with an introduction or overview of the booklet as well as a series of specific learning objectives to give a purpose to the study of the LIFEPAC. The introduction and objectives are followed by a vocabulary section which may be found at the beginning of each section at the lower levels or in the glossary at the high school level. Vocabulary words are used to develop word recognition and should not be confused with the spelling words introduced later in the LIFEPAC. The student should learn all vocabulary words before working the LIFEPAC sections to improve comprehension, retention, and reading skills.

Each activity or written assignment in grades 2 through 12 has a number for easy identification, such as 1.1. The first number corresponds to the LIFEPAC section and the number to the right of the decimal is the number of the activity.

Teacher checkpoints, which are essential to maintain quality learning, are found at various locations throughout the LIFEPAC. The teacher should check 1) neatness of work and penmanship, 2) quality of understanding (tested with a short oral quiz), 3) thoroughness of answers (complete sentences and paragraphs, correct spelling, etc.), 4) completion of activities (no blank spaces), and 5) accuracy of answers as compared to the answer key (all answers correct).

The self test questions in grades 2 through 12 are also number coded for easy reference. For example, 2.015 means that this is the 15th question in the self test of Section 2. The first number corresponds to the LIFEPAC section, the zero indicates that it is a self test question, and the number to the right of the zero the question number.

The LIFEPAC test is packaged at the center of each LIFEPAC. It should be removed and put aside before giving the booklet to the student for study.

Answer and test keys in grades 2 through 12 have the same numbering system as the LIFEPACs and appear throughout this guide. The student may be given access to the answer keys (not the test keys) under teacher supervision so that he can score his own work.

A thorough study of the Scope & Sequence by the teacher before instruction begins is essential to the success of the student. The teacher should become familiar with expected skill mastery and understand how these grade-level skills fit into the overall skill development of the curriculum. The teacher should also preview the objectives that appear at the beginning of each LIFEPAC for additional preparation and planning.

TEST SCORING AND GRADING

Answer keys and test keys give examples of correct answers. They convey the idea, but the student may use many ways to express a correct answer. The teacher should check for the essence of the answer, not for the exact wording. Many questions are high level and require thinking and creativity on the part of the student. Each answer should be scored based on whether or not the main idea written by the student matches the model example. "Any Order" or "Either Order" in a key indicates that no particular order is necessary to be correct.

Most self tests and LIFEPAC tests at the lower elementary levels are scored at 1 point per answer; however, the upper levels may have a point system awarding 2 to 5 points for various answers or questions. Further, the total test points will vary; they may not always equal 100 points. They may be 78, 85, 100, 105, etc.

Example 1

Teacher Check

Initial Date

Example 2

Teacher Check

Initial Date

A score box similar to ex. 1 above is located at the end of each self test and on the front of the LIFEPAC test. The bottom score, 72, represents the total number of points possible on the test. The upper score, 58, represents the number of points your student will need to receive an 80% or passing grade. If you wish to establish the exact percentage that your student has achieved, find the total points of his correct answers and divide it by the bottom number (in this case 72). For example, if your student has a point total of 65, divide 65 by 72 for a grade of 90%. Referring to ex. 2, on a test with a total of 105 possible points, the student would have to receive a minimum of 84 correct points for an 80% or passing grade. If your student has received 93 points, simply divide the 93 by 105 for a percentage grade of 89%. Students who receive a score below 80% should review the LIFEPAC and retest using the appropriate Alternate Test found in the Teacher's Guide.

The following is a guideline to assign letter grades for completed LIFEPACs based on a maximum total score of 100 points.

Example:

LIFEPAC Test	=	60% of the Total Score (or percent grade)
Self Test	=	25% of the Total Score (average percent of self tests)
Reports	=	10% or 10* points per LIFEPAC
Oral Work	=	5% or 5* points per LIFEPAC

*Determined by the teacher's subjective evaluation of the student's daily work.

Example:

LIFEPAC Test Score	=	92%	92 × .60	=	55 points
Self Test Average	=	90%	90 × .25	=	23 points
Reports				=	8 points
Oral Work				=	4 points
TOTAL POINTS				=	90 points

Grade Scale based on point system:

100 – 94	=	A
93 – 86	=	B
85 – 77	=	C
76 – 70	=	D
Below 70	=	F

TEACHER HINTS AND STUDYING TECHNIQUES

LIFEPAC activities are written to check the level of understanding of the preceding text. The student may look back to the text as necessary to complete these activities; however, a student should never attempt to do the activities without reading (studying) the text first. Self tests and LIFEPAC tests are never open-book tests.

Language arts activities (skill integration) often appear within other subject curriculum. The purpose is to give the student an opportunity to test his skill mastery outside of the context in which it was presented.

Writing complete answers (paragraphs) to some questions is an integral part of the LIFEPAC curriculum in all subjects. This builds communication and organization skills, increases understanding and retention of ideas, and helps enforce good penmanship. Complete sentences should be encouraged for this type of activity. Obviously, single words or phrases do not meet the intent of the activity, since multiple lines are given for the response.

Review is essential to student success. Time invested in review where review is suggested will be time saved in correcting errors later. Self tests, unlike the section activities, are closed book. This procedure helps to identify weaknesses before they become too great to overcome. Certain objectives from self tests are cumulative and test previous sections; therefore, good preparation for a self test must include all material studied up to that testing point.

The following procedure checklist has been found to be successful in developing good study habits in the LIFEPAC curriculum.

1. Read the introduction and Table of Contents.
2. Read the objectives.
3. Recite and study the entire vocabulary (glossary) list.
4. Study each section as follows:
    a. Read the introduction and study the section objectives.
    b. Read all the text for the entire section, but answer none of the activities.
    c. Return to the beginning of the section and memorize each vocabulary word and definition.
    d. Reread the section, complete the activities, check the answers with the answer key, correct all errors, and have the teacher check.
    e. Read the self test but do not answer the questions.
    f. Go to the beginning of the first section and reread the text and answers to the activities up to the self test you have not yet done.
    g. Answer the questions to the self test without looking back.
    h. Have the self test checked by the teacher.
    i. Correct the self test and have the teacher check the corrections.
    j. Repeat steps a–i for each section.
5. Use the **SQ3R** method to prepare for the LIFEPAC test.

    Scan the whole LIFEPAC.
    Question yourself on the objectives.
    Read the whole LIFEPAC again.
    Recite through an oral examination.
    Review weak areas.
6. Take the LIFEPAC test as a closed-book test.
7. LIFEPAC tests are administered and scored under direct teacher supervision. Students who receive scores below 80% should review the LIFEPAC using the **SQ3R** study method and take the Alternate Test located in the Teacher's Guide. The final test grade may be the grade on the Alternate Test or an average of the grades from the original LIFEPAC test and the Alternate Test.

GOAL SETTING AND SCHEDULES

Each school must develop its own schedule, because no single set of procedures will fit every situation. The following is an example of a daily schedule that includes the five LIFEPAC subjects as well as time slotted for special activities.

Possible Daily Schedule

8:15	-	8:25	Pledges, prayer, songs, devotions, etc.
8:25	-	9:10	Bible
9:10	-	9:55	Language Arts
9:55	-	10:15	Recess (juice break)
10:15	-	11:00	Math
11:00	-	11:45	History & Geography
11:45	-	12:30	Lunch, recess, quiet time
12:30	-	1:15	Science
1:15	-		Drill, remedial work, enrichment*

***Enrichment:** *Computer time, physical education, field trips, fun reading, games and puzzles, family business, hobbies, resource persons, guests, crafts, creative work, electives, music appreciation, projects.*

Basically, two factors need to be considered when assigning work to a student in the LIFEPAC curriculum.

The first is time. An average of 45 minutes should be devoted to each subject, each day. Remember, this is only an average. Because of extenuating circumstances, a student may spend only 15 minutes on a subject one day and the next day spend 90 minutes on the same subject.

The second factor is the number of pages to be worked in each subject. A single LIFEPAC is designed to take three to four weeks to complete. Allowing about three to four days for LIFEPAC introduction, review, and tests, the student has approximately 15 days to complete the LIFEPAC pages. Simply take the number of pages in the LIFEPAC, divide it by 15 and you will have the number of pages that must be completed on a daily basis to keep the student on schedule. For example, a LIFEPAC containing 45 pages will require three completed pages per day. Again, this is only an average. While working a 45-page LIFEPAC, the student may complete only one page the first day if the text has a lot of activities or reports, but go on to complete five pages the next day.

Long-range planning requires some organization. Because the traditional school year originates in the early fall of one year and continues to late spring of the following year, a calendar should be devised that covers this period of time. Approximate beginning and completion dates can be noted on the calendar as well as special occasions such as holidays, vacations and birthdays. Since each LIFEPAC takes three to four weeks or 18 days to complete, it should take about 180 school days to finish a set of 10 LIFEPACs. Starting at the beginning school date, mark off 18 school days on the calendar and that will become the targeted completion date for the first LIFEPAC. Continue marking the calendar until you have established dates for the remaining nine LIFEPACs making adjustments for previously noted holidays and vacations. If all five subjects are being used, the ten established target dates should be the same for the LIFEPACs in each subject.

TEACHING SUPPLEMENTS

The sample weekly lesson plan and student grading sheet forms are included in this section as teacher support materials and may be duplicated at the convenience of the teacher.

The student grading sheet is provided for those who desire to follow the suggested guidelines for assignment of letter grades as previously discussed. The student's self test scores should be posted as percentage grades. When the LIFEPAC is completed, the teacher should average the self test grades, multiply the average by .25, and post the points in the box marked self test points. The LIFEPAC percentage grade should be multiplied by .60 and posted. Next, the teacher should award and post points for written reports and oral work. A report may be any type of written work assigned to the student whether it is a LIFEPAC or additional learning activity. Oral work includes the student's ability to respond orally to questions which may or may not be related to LIFEPAC activities or any type of oral report assigned by the teacher. The points may then be totaled and a final grade entered along with the date that the LIFEPAC was completed.

The Student Record Book which was specifically designed for use with the Alpha Omega curriculum provides space to record weekly progress for one student over a nine-week period as well as a place to post self test and LIFEPAC scores. The Student Record Books are available through the current Alpha Omega catalog; however, unlike the enclosed forms these books are not for duplication and should be purchased in sets of four to cover a full academic year.

This section of the language arts Teacher's Guide also includes a *Book Report Form*, a *Books Read Chart*, a *Phonics Rules* chart, the *Index of Concepts*, and a *Suggested Reading List*.

The Book Report Form and the Books Read Chart may be duplicated for individual student use.

The Phonics Rules chart notes the unit where specific phonics concepts are first covered in Language Arts 2.

The Index of Concepts is a quick reference guide for the teacher who may be looking for a rule or explanation that applies to a particular concept. It does not identify each use of the concept in the various LIFEPACs. The concepts change by grade level with the emphasis on phonics and reading skills for younger students changing to spelling and grammar for the older students.

A suggested reading list has also been included. It is not necessary that you use these exact books but the list can be used as a guideline for selecting other books that will be appropriate.

WEEKLY LESSON PLANNER

Week of:

Monday	Subject	Subject	Subject	Subject
Tuesday	Subject	Subject	Subject	Subject
Wednesday	Subject	Subject	Subject	Subject
Thursday	Subject	Subject	Subject	Subject
Friday	Subject	Subject	Subject	Subject

WEEKLY LESSON PLANNER

Week of:

Monday	Subject	Subject	Subject	Subject
Tuesday	Subject	Subject	Subject	Subject
Wednesday	Subject	Subject	Subject	Subject
Thursday	Subject	Subject	Subject	Subject
Friday	Subject	Subject	Subject	Subject

Student Name ______________________ Year ______________

Bible

LP	Self Test Scores by Sections 1	2	3	4	5	Self Test Points	LIFEPAC Test	Oral Points	Report Points	Final Grade	Date
01											
02											
03											
04											
05											
06											
07											
08											
09											
10											

History & Geography

LP	Self Test Scores by Sections 1	2	3	4	5	Self Test Points	LIFEPAC Test	Oral Points	Report Points	Final Grade	Date
01											
02											
03											
04											
05											
06											
07											
08											
09											
10											

Language Arts

LP	Self Test Scores by Sections 1	2	3	4	5	Self Test Points	LIFEPAC Test	Oral Points	Report Points	Final Grade	Date
01											
02											
03											
04											
05											
06											
07											
08											
09											
10											

Student Name ______________________ Year ____________

Math

LP	Self Test Scores by Sections 1	2	3	4	5	Self Test Points	LIFEPAC Test	Oral Points	Report Points	Final Grade	Date
01											
02											
03											
04											
05											
06											
07											
08											
09											
10											

Science

LP	Self Test Scores by Sections 1	2	3	4	5	Self Test Points	LIFEPAC Test	Oral Points	Report Points	Final Grade	Date
01											
02											
03											
04											
05											
06											
07											
08											
09											
10											

Spelling/Electives

LP	Self Test Scores by Sections 1	2	3	4	5	Self Test Points	LIFEPAC Test	Oral Points	Report Points	Final Grade	Date
01											
02											
03											
04											
05											
06											
07											
08											
09											
10											

BOOK REPORT FORM

Title ______________________________ Your Name ______________________________

Author ______________________________ Date ______________________________

Illustrator ______________________________ Principal Characters ______________________________

Number of Pages ______________________________ ______________________________

Copyright Date ______________________________ ______________________________

Fiction or Nonfiction ______________________________ Setting ______________________________

Summary:

A summary gives the important events of a story or book. It skips most of the details but a few make the report more interesting. The summary should be written in complete sentences.

____

____

____

____

____

____

____

____

____

____

____

____

____

Tell why you did or did not like the book.

____

____

____

____

____

____

____

Name: ______________________________

Books Read

Title: Author: Date:	Title: Author: Date:	Title: Author: Date:	Title: Author: Date:
Title: Author: Date:	Title: Author: Date:	Title: Author: Date:	Title: Author: Date:
Title: Author: Date:	Title: Author: Date:	Title: Author: Date:	Title: Author: Date:
Title: Author: Date:	Title: Author: Date:	Title: Author: Date:	Title: Author: Date:
Title: Author: Date:	Title: Author: Date:	Title: Author: Date:	Title: Author: Date:
Title: Author: Date:	Title: Author: Date:	Title: Author: Date:	Title: Author: Date:
Title: Author: Date:	Title: Author: Date:	Title: Author: Date:	Title: Author: Date:
Title: Author: Date:	Title: Author: Date:	Title: Author: Date:	Title: Author: Date:
Title: Author: Date:	Title: Author: Date:	Title: Author: Date:	Title: Author: Date:

PHONICS RULES

The following letter and letter combinations are introduced in Language Arts 100 and continue through LA 200. **The LIFEPAC is noted where the rule is specifically addressed.**

a e i o u
b c d f g h j k l m n p q r s t v w x y z
th wh sh ch, ng nk, ck mb lk gn kn gh
ar er ir or ur, ai ay, au aw, ei ey, ea ee, ie
oa, oo, ew, ou, ow, oi, oy
gh ph, igh

	Rule		Example	LIFEPAC
1.	short vowels (cvc)	-	*a* (bat) *e* (bet) *i* (bit) *o* (cot) *u* (but)	201
2.	long vowels (cvcv)	-	*a* (wave) *e* (Pete) *i* (tire) *o* (bone) *u* (use)	201
3.	long vowels (cvvc)	-	*a* (nail) *e* (seal) *i* (tied) *o* (boat) *u* (suit)	201
4.	c and g	-	hard sound before *a, o, u*	207
		-	soft sound before *e, i*	207
5.	q (qu)	-	always has the sound of *kw*	
6.	y	-	as *y* (yard)	
		-	as *e* (baby)	
		-	as *i* (cry)	
7.	consonant digraphs	-	*th, wh, sh, ch*	204
8.	special blends	-	*nk* (sank)	203
		-	*ng* (sing)	204
9.	silent consonants	-	*ck* (lock)	204
		-	*mb* (lamb), *lk* (talk), *gn* (sign)	207
		-	*kn* (know), *gh* (though), *t* (often)	207
10.	r-controlled vowels	-	*ar* (car) *or* (for)	203
		-	*er* (her), *ir* (sir), *ur* (fur)	203
11.	vowel digraphs	-	*ai* as long *a* (fail)	201
		-	*ea, ee* as long *e* (beat) (feet)	201
		-	*ie* as long *i* (pie)	201
		-	*oa* as long *o* (boat)	201
		-	*ue* as long *oo* sound (clue)	201
		-	*ay* as long *a* (pray)	202
		-	*ey* as long *e* (donkey)	202
		-	*uy* as long *i* (guy)	202
		-	*au* (cause), *aw* (saw)	202
		-	short *oo* sound (book)	202
		-	long *oo* sound (zoo)	202
		-	*ew* as long *u* (few)	202
		-	*ou* as long *u* (soup)	205
		-	as *ow* (cloud)*	205
		-	*ow* as long *o* (slow)	205
		-	*ow* as *ow* (clown)*	205
		-	*oi, oy* (boil) (boy)*	205
12.	letter groups	-	*gh, ph* as *f* (laugh) (phone)	207
		-	*igh* as long *i* (sigh)	207

* sometimes referred to as diphthongs

INDEX OF CONCEPTS

SUGGESTED READING LIST

YOU ARE SPECIAL:

Max Lucado:
Just In Case You Ever Wonder
Because I Love You

Lois Lowry and Middy Thomas:
Gooney Bird Greene (story writing and telling)

Harriet Ziefert:
First He Made the Sun (kids could illustrate this book)

POETRY BOOKS:

Lee Bennett Hopkins:
Good Books, Good Times

Douglas Florian:
Bow Wow Meow Meow: It's Rhyming Cats and Dogs

James Stevenson:
Com Chowder

100 DAYS CELEBRATION:

Rosemary Wells:
Emily's First 100 Days of School

Brenda Haugen:
The 100th Day of School

HOLIDAYS/CELEBRATIONS:

Deborah Chancellor:
Celebration Days! Holidays Around the World (DK Reader)

Tasha Tudor:
A Time to Keep: The Tasha Tudor Book of Holidays

WRITING LETTERS:

Alma Flor Ada:
Dear Peter Rabbit

Janet and Allan Ahlberg:
The Jolly Postman
The Jolly Christmas Postman

Holly Hobbie:
Toot and Puddle

Annette Langen:
Letters From Felix: A Little Rabbit on a World Tour

Beatrix Potter:
Dear Peter Rabbit: A Story with Real Miniature Letters

Sarah Stewart:
The Gardner

Eileen Christelow:
Letters From a Desperate Dog

ANIMALS/FABLES:

Seymour Simon:
Animal Fact/Animal Fiction

Judith Walker Hodge:
Animal Hospital (DK Reader)

Peter Spier:
Noah's Ark

Don Daily:
The Classic Treasury of Aesop's Fables

Arnold Lobel:
Fables

Melvin Berger:
Look Out for Turtles!

SPORTS:

Kathryn Cristaldi:
Baseball Ballerina

Leonard Kessler:
Here Comes the Strikeout

Jean Marzollo:
Soccer Sam

Peggy Parish:
Play Ball, Amelia Bedelia

WRITING/ILLUSTRATING BOOK:

Eileen Christelow:
What Do Authors Do?

Eileen Christelow:
What Do Illustrators Do?

INSTRUCTIONS FOR LANGUAGE ARTS

The LIFEPAC curriculum from grades two through twelve is structured so that the daily instructional material is written directly into the LIFEPACs. The student is encouraged to read and follow this instructional material in order to develop independent study habits. The teacher should introduce the LIFEPAC to the student, set a required completion schedule, complete teacher checks, be available for questions regarding both content and procedures, administer and grade tests, and develop additional learning activities as desired. Teachers working with several students may schedule their time so that students are assigned to a quiet work activity when it is necessary to spend instructional time with one particular student.

Language arts includes those subjects that develop the students' communication skills. The LIFEPAC approach to combining reading, spelling, penmanship, composition, grammar, speech, and literature in a single unit allows the teacher to integrate the study of these various language arts subject areas. The variety and scope of the curriculum may make it difficult for students to complete the required material within the suggested daily scheduled time of 45 minutes. Spelling, book reports, and various forms of composition may need to be completed during the afternoon enrichment period.

Cursive handwriting is introduced in the second grade LIFEPAC 208 with regular practice following in succeeding LIFEPACs. Diacritical markings are introduced in LIFEPAC 207. A pronunciation key with basic diacritical markings is provided, and section sight words include diacritical markings once the pronunciation key has been introduced.

Spelling tests contained in the Teacher's Guide are final spelling tests and should be administered with each Language Arts LIFEPAC test.

Many homonyms such as "piece" and "peace" are dependent on meaning for correct spelling. By placing the spelling words in sentences, the spelling tests simplify the teacher's work of properly presenting the correct words from the LIFEPAC spelling lists.

The materials section refers only to LIFEPAC materials and does not include materials which may be needed for the additional learning activities. Additional learning activities provide a change from the daily school routine, encourage the student's interest in learning, and may be used as a reward for good study habits.

Teacher Resources Section. This section is in the back of this guide. It include the following items:

1. Section-by-section and cumulative lists of the spelling words covered in this course.
2. Word Families manipulatives that can be reproduced on cardstock.
3. Numbered penmanship paper for the spelling tests can be made from the reproducible masters. Other paper with guidelines can also be used for the spelling tests.

LANGUAGE ARTS 201

Unit 1: Know Your Nouns

TEACHER NOTES

MATERIALS NEEDED FOR LIFEPAC	
Required	Suggested
• sharp pencil • scissors	• crayons or colored pencils • mirror (or baby & recent photographs of student) • manuscript alphabet chart • notebook or composition book for journalizing • magazines (for cutting out pictures) • glue or glue stick • paper with guidelines for Spelling Tests*

* It is suggested that students use paper with guidelines when taking Spelling Tests. An optional reproducible master for the "spelling paper" referred to in the LIFEPACs is in the Teacher Resources section of this Teacher's Guide.

OPTIONAL ADDITIONAL LEARNING ACTIVITIES

This unit begins by reminding the students of how special God created all people. We are made in His image! He has a special plan for us! Reading the book *Just in Case You Ever Wonder* by Max Lucado would be a good introduction to this unit.

Section 1

1. Discuss these questions with the student(s).
   a. How are people alike?
   b. How are people different from each other?
   c. How do you know if someone is happy?
   d. How do you know if someone is sad?
2. Discuss the differences between animals and people.
   Write these phrases on the board:

   Can't pray to God
   Know right & wrong
   Need to sleep
   Made by God
   Can't read the Bible
   Can believe in Jesus

Guide the students to put these phrases in a simple Venn diagram:

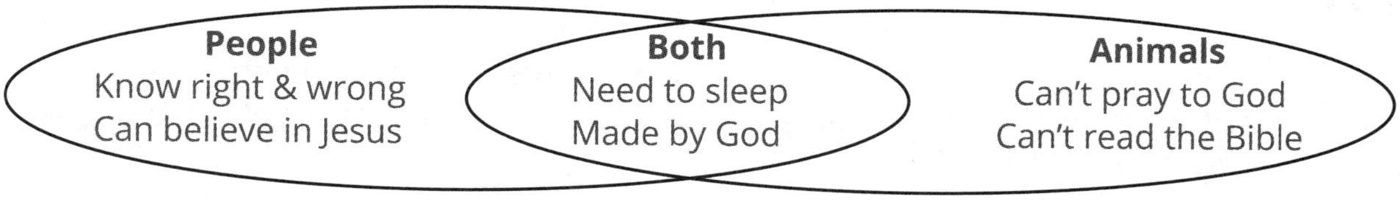

3. Tell the students to look at themselves in a mirror. (Or students could look at a photo of themselves.) Help them describe themselves verbally. Have students write these descriptions in their journal. (Teacher or parent could add their own comments on the journal page.)
4. Compare baby photographs of the students with recent photographs. Discuss with the student how they have changed and grown. Discuss with them all the things that they can do now versus with what they could do when they were babies.
5. Read Genesis 1:26–13 to the students. Discuss with them how we are made in the image of God. Tell them of the responsibilities we have from God to be good stewards of this world.
6. Find the students' meaning of their names. Discuss the meaning of their names or if they are named after someone special. Tell them that Jesus knows their names (you may want to refer to John 10:1–16).

Art Activity:

Print out students' names using software such as Word Art (or write the students' names on paper). Let students color and decorate their names.

Section 2

1. Students may make a collage poster of the three categories of nouns:
   Persons; Places; Things (pictures may be cut from magazines and glued in the correct boxes).

Nouns

Persons	Places	Things

2. Play the game "Telephone" with students, reminding them that it is important to be good listeners.
3. Listen for the beginning, middle, ending consonant sounds. Have the students use consonant flashcards to show you the *beginning* consonant sound that is heard of these words that you say to them:

dog	pig
fish	donkey
zebra	rooster

   Have the students use consonant flashcards to show you the ending consonant sound that is heard of these words that you say to them:

cat	sheep
bread	fork
muffin	petal

   Have the students use consonant flashcards to show you the middle consonant sound that is heard of these words that you say to them:

cabin	camel
donut	hotel
robin	woman

Section 3

1. Play this "listening, remembering" game: Students take turns listing what they would take on a picnic. The list must go alphabetically. The first person says, "I am going on a picnic and will take an apple." The second person must think of a word that begins with the letter *b* and then will say: "I am going on a picnic and will take an apple and banana." The third person must think of a word that begins with the letter *c* and then will say: "I am going on a picnic and will take an apple, banana, and carrot," etc. See if you can get all the way through the entire alphabet!
2. Write these words on the board or a large piece of paper:

   Silver Lake, Rock River, New York, Jane, Mark, Mars, Spot

   (Or you may write names of a lake, river, city, girl, boy, pet, etc. that are familiar to students.) Ask the students how these words are alike. Tell the students to notice that there is a capital letter at the beginning of these names. Ask the students how they write their name. Discuss with them why capital letters are used for names. Remind them that these names are called *proper nouns*.
3. Find a short human interest story in a newspaper or magazine that includes some names/proper nouns. Read the article together and find the proper nouns.
4. Listen to, sing, or read the words of the song "If I Were a Butterfly" by Brian M. Howard (Copyright © 1974, 2002 Mission Hills Music, www.ButterflySong.com, All rights reserved. [BMI]). Discuss with the children how creation praises God. Guide the discussion to how they can praise God.

Suggested Books:

I Like Myself! by Karen Beaumont
Amazing Grace by Mary Hoffman
Tacky the Penguin by Helen Lester
You are Special by Max Lucado
The Ugly Duckling by Hans Christian Andersen & Jerry Pinkney

Journal Suggestions:

1. Write the following poem on the board or a large piece of paper. Tell the students to write the poem in their journal. Remind the students to include the date on the journal entry.

   I'm as happy as can be
   That my God created me.

   God made me so uniquely
   There is no one just like me.

   Thank you God for making me
   And loving me so perfectly.

2. Discuss the meaning of the phrase "apple of my eye." Tell the students that God loves us and we are the apple of God's eye. Write Psalm 17:8 on the board or a large piece of paper, and tell the students to write this verse in their journal. (You can add apple stickers or drawings of an apple with the verse!)

   Keep me as the **apple** of the eye
   hide me under the shadow of thy wings.
   Psalm 17:8

3. This is a little twist on the journaling—you as the teacher can write in the students' journals about the student: what you think makes them special, some talents that you notice that they have, etc.

» WORKSHEET ANSWERS

Spelling Words 1-1

1. trip
2. went
3. sit
4. bad
5. hot
6. fast
7. its
8. tell
9. best
10. wish

Spelling Words 1-3

1. f
2. h
3. d
4. i
5. l
6. b
7. k
8. a
9. g
10. e
11. j
12. c

Administer the LIFEPAC Spelling Test.
The test is provided in this Teacher's Guide.
Evaluate the tests and review the words the students spelled incorrectly.
If necessary, review all of the words in the unit to prepare for the alternate spelling test.
Administer the Alternate LIFEPAC Spelling test that is provided in this Teacher's Guide.

Administer the LIFEPAC Test.
The test is to be administered in one session. Give no help except with directions.
Evaluate the tests and review areas where the students have done poorly.
Review the pages and activities that stress the concepts tested.
If necessary, administer the Alternate LIFEPAC Test.

SPELLING WORDS 1-1 ACTIVITY

Choose the word that best completes each sentence and write it on the lines.

bad	fast	best	hot	its	sit
tell	trip	us	went	wish	yet

1. April and Lee took a ______________ to their uncle's cabin.

2. They ______________ on a train.

3. April got to ______________ by the window.

4. Lee felt ______________ that he could not sit by the window.

5. It was ______________ because the sun was shining brightly.

6. The train went very ______________ through the country.

7. The train stayed on ______________ track.

8. April wanted to ______________ their uncle about the train trip.

9. It was the ______________ trip ever!

10. April and Lee ______________ they could go on another trip.

SPELLING WORDS 1-3 ACTIVITY

Match the spelling word with its meaning.

1.	________	coat	**a.**	a bucket
2.	________	float	**b.**	gentle, humble
3.	________	goes	**c.**	special coat with trousers or skirt
4.	________	green	**d.**	present tense of moves or travels
5.	________	mean	**e.**	to understand the meaning of written words
6.	________	meek	**f.**	outer clothing with long sleeves, jacket
7.	________	need	**g.**	water that falls from clouds in the sky
8.	________	pail	**h.**	to move on top of water or air
9.	________	rain	**i.**	the color of most plants, grass, and leaves
10.	________	read	**j.**	time of rest for mind and body
11.	________	sleep	**k.**	lack of something required
12.	________	suit	**l.**	not kind, cruel

ANSWER KEYS

SECTION 1

1.1 – 1.7 Teacher check

1.8 Possible answers:
- a. bad, hot
- b. fast, best
- c. best, fast
- d. hot, bad
- e. its
- f. sit
- g. tell
- h. trip
- i. us
- j. went, wish
- k. wish, went
- l. yet

1.9 h(a)t b(e)d p(i)g m(o)p c(u)p
p(a)n p(e)n f(i)n c(o)t s(u)n

1.10 c(u)b~~e~~ r(a)k~~e~~ b(o)n~~e~~ f(i)v~~e~~ w(a)v~~e~~
P(e)t~~e~~ b(i)k~~e~~ n(o)s~~e~~ t(i)r~~e~~ v(a)s~~e~~

1.11 s(e)~~a~~l r(a)~~i~~n j(e)~~e~~p s(u)~~i~~t s(o)~~a~~p
b(o)~~a~~t n(a)~~i~~l l(e)~~a~~f p(a)~~i~~l f(e)~~e~~t

1.12 Teacher check

1.13 Any order:
baby, doctor, grandma

1.14 Any order:
kitchen, park, city

1.15 Any order:
monkey, cow, tiger

1.16 Any order:
glass, pizza, paper

1.17 Teacher check
- a. The (family) went to the (mountains).
- b. The (children) played (games) in the (car).
- c. (Mother) and (Father) hiked in the (mountains).
- d. (Mother) liked the beautiful (flowers).
- e. (Brother) rode his (bike) on the (trails).
- f. (Sister) walked with the (dog).
- g. The (dog) barked and wagged its (tail).
- h. The (children) did not want to go (home).
- i. The (brother) and (sister) slept in the (car).
- j. They told their (friends) about the (mountains).

1.18

yet	wish
its (*or* sit)	best
bad	fast
sit (*or* its)	trip
us	tell
hot	went

1.19 Suggested answers:
- a. Christmas
- b. Christmas shopping
- c. an old teddy bear
- d. her brother
- e. in the park
- f. in the bicycle basket
- g. a teddy bear
- h. a hug

1.20 Teacher check

1.21 Teacher check

1.22 Any order under each category:

CVC	**CVCV**	**CVCC**
web	cone	meat
yet	hole	goat
rag	tape	beep
zip	bite	wait
job	cube	leap
cab	vine	tail
fox	wave	foam

1.23 kite, string, cloth, sticks, mom, glue, scissors, table, kite, hill, kite, sky

1.24 Teacher check

1.25 Circled words:
Circus, Alex, Kelly, store, Dad, poster, circus, pictures, tigers, lions, monkeys, clowns, acrobats, poster, circus, Dad

family, bus, circus, animals, tricks, monkey, bike, clowns, clothes, clown, bike, bell, lions, girl, Alex, Kelly, candy, sodas, Mom, pictures, home, Mom, Dad, circus

1.26 Teacher check

SELF TEST 1

1.01 noun

1.02 a. teacher
b. house
c. book
d. man
e. zoo
f. moon

1.03 Any order within categories:

a. *cvc*	b. *cvvc*	c. *cvcv*
bed	soap	nose
fin	leaf	tire
mop	jeep	kite
pig	rain	five

1.04 image
1.05 words
1.06 words
1.07 writer
1.08 picture
1.09 artist

SECTION 2

2.1 Possible answers:
a. five, line, tune
b. line, five, tune
c. joke
d. gave
e. made, sale, ride
f. these
g. sale, made, ride
h. name, nice
i. nice, name
j. ride, made, sale
k. tune, five, line
l. write

2.2 a. – f. Teacher check
2.3 Teacher check
2.4 Circled letters:
b r p
f f m

2.5 Word search:

n	b	s	d	p	u	k	w	h	g	m
a	i	l	t	h	e	s	e	b	y	a
m	t	r	q	j	o	k	e	n	b	d
e	d	i	u	y	e	r	f	i	v	e
o	m	d	g	a	v	e	g	z	l	x
c	x	e	f	q	p	v	l	e	i	w
t	w	r	i	t	e	k	i	j	m	r
s	a	l	e	c	j	a	n	i	c	e
h	n	v	o	t	u	n	e	f	s	z

2.6 Any order:
paper
truck
factory
pulp
book
tree

2.7 Any order:
pencils
trees
logs
machines
books
notebooks
newspapers
things

2.8
a. dogs
b. farms
c. tigers
d. playgrounds
e. parrots
f. rivers
g. boys
h. pencils
i. girls
j. pizzas
k. teachers
l. socks

2.9
a. lion
b. park
c. bear
d. lake
e. shark
f. hill
g. doctor
h. book
i. farmer
j. bean
k. sister
l. shirt

2.10 Teacher check
2.11 Teacher check
2.12 Teacher check
2.13 Circled letters:
l n t
m n t

SELF TEST 2

2.01 noun
2.02 singular
2.03 plural
2.04 s
2.05 girl, horse
2.06 girl, horse, forest
2.07 horse, river
2.08 horse, water
2.09 skunk, girl, horse
2.010 horse, girl, home

2.011
a. stamps
b. frogs
c. arms
d. cars
e. balls
f. barns
g. roads
h. forks

2.012
a. map
b. toad
c. muffin
d. spoon
e. bug
f. leg
g. paper
h. flag

2.013 g
2.014 n
2.015 t

SECTION 3

3.1 Possible answers:
a. need, meek, read, coat, suit
b. float
c. goes
d. green
e. rain, mean
f. read, coat, suit, meek, need
g. coat, read, suit, meek, need
h. pail
i. mean, rain
j. meek, coat, need, read, suit
k. sleep
l. suit, read, coat, meek, need

3.2 Teacher check – Student answers will vary

3.3 Suggested answers:
a. boy, man
b. girl, woman
c. dog, pet
d. state
e. store
f. city, town

3.4 Teacher check

3.5 Circled words:
Kay's, Kay, Kay, April, July, Johnson's Pet Shop, Dillon
Kay, Beaver River
Fluffy, Socks, Mr. Johnson, Monday
Kay, Johnson's Pet Shop, Main Street, Dillon
Kay, Sara, Kay
Kay, Fluffy
Mr. Johnson, Kay, Fluffy

3.6

need	float
coat	meek
read	goes
rain	green
suit	mean
sleep	pall

3.7 g p t
n r m
z v

3.8 Teacher check

3.9 Teacher check

3.10 with a capital letter

3.11
a. cats
b. lions
c. cups
d. crayons
e. books
f. brothers

3.12
a. tiger
b. river
c. teacher
d. chair
e. paper
f. toy

3.13 Teacher check

3.14 Student answers – Teacher check

3.15

Circled words:	Correct spelling:
a. beest	best
b. gaiv	gave
c. faste	fast
d. grean	green
e. mene	mean
f. naem	name
g. nise	nice
h. tripp	trip
i. rane	rain
j. theze	these
k. wint	went
l. sute	suit

3.16 sit, its

3.17 mean, name

3.18 amen

SELF TEST 3

3.01 – 3.07 Student answers – Answers will vary
3.08 state
3.09 city, town
3.010 girl, woman
3.011 boy, man
3.012 lake
3.013 sea
Suggested answers – any three, any order:
3.014 eyes are watching
3.015 ears are hearing
3.016 lips are silent
hands are still
feet are still

UNIT REVIEW

1. h
2. u
3. R D
4. Circled words:
pan, hat, map
5. Circled words:
rake, kite, wave
6. b(o)~~a~~t n(a)~~i~~l l(e)~~a~~f
7. Circled words:
river, mother, cat
8. Circled words:
Boston, Mary, Silver Lake
9. a. (boy) (cat)
b. (cat) ~~kittens~~
c. (dog) ~~kittens~~
d. (cat) (dog)
e. ~~girls~~ (kitten)
10. k t r (or b)
11. g n m
12. n k p
13. reading writing speaking
14. Student answer – Teacher check

LIFEPAC TEST

1. a e i o u

2. a. rabbit b. fish
c. pumpkin d. mittens

3. a. clown b. lemon
c. football d. fork

4. a. tiger b. peanut
c. woman d. music

5. Any order:

a.	b.	c.
pig	boat	five
pan	seal	nose
bed	nail	cake

6. a. dog
b. boy
c. cat
d. lion

7. Student answers

8. a. state
b. girl, woman
c. dog, pet
d. city

9. Any three, any order:
a. reading
b. writing
c. speaking
listening

10. a. stamps b. frogs
c. balls d. barns

11. a. map b. toad
c. muffin d. bug
e. leg

ALTERNATE LIFEPAC TEST

1. a. o
b. a
c. u
d. e
e. i

2. a. pig b. bike
c. doll d. fork
e. nine

3. a. rabbit b. book
c. spoon d. six
e. pencil

4. a. paper b. river
c. woman d. shovel
e. tiger

5. Any order within categories:

a.	b.	c.
dog	goat	nine
pot	bean	fine
wig	sail	bake

6. a. rooster b. boy
c. girl d. fish

7. a. bug b. flag
c. map d. frog

8. a. rivers b. girls
c. beds d. nails

9. a. river b. teacher
c. state d. girl

10. a. Salt Lake b. Denver
c. Ron d. Target

11. Any three, any order:
a. reading
b. writing
c. speaking
listening

12. So you can learn many things and learn more about God.

SPELLING TEST

1	name	Do you have your **name** on your Spelling Test?	name
2	write	Please remember to **write** neatly!	write
3	green	The **green** bicycle is new.	green
4	sale	That puppy is not for **sale**.	sale
5	made	Grandmother **made** the birthday cake.	made
6	five	There were **five** candles on the birthday cake.	five
7	wish	She made a **wish** after she blew out the candles.	wish
8	rain	It began to **rain** after the birthday party.	rain
9	sleep	It was not easy going to **sleep**.	sleep
10	read	We will **read** the book together.	read
11	fast	The cheetah can run **fast**.	fast
12	goes	Michael **goes** to swimming lessons every day.	goes
13	hot	The stove is **hot**.	hot
14	float	We like to **float** on the lake.	float
15	tell	I want to **tell** you a secret.	tell
16	sit	The cat likes to **sit** on your lap.	sit
17	joke	They laughed at my **joke**.	joke
18	suit	Dad wears a **suit** to work.	suit
19	trip	We are going on a **trip** this summer.	trip
20	yet	It isn't time for supper **yet**.	yet

LANGUAGE ARTS 201

ALTERNATE LIFEPAC TEST

Name ______________________

Date ______________________

My Score

42 / 53

Each answer = 1 point

Circle the vowel in each row of letters.

1.

a. g h k l o

b. j q c a m

c. w x u f b

d. z e c p s

e. i d n r t

Circle the beginning consonants of the words.

2.

a. pig b. bike

c. doll d. fork

e. nine

Circle the ending consonants of the words.

3. a. rabbit b. book

c. spoon d. six

e. pencil

Circle the middle consonants of the words.

4. a. paper b. river

c. woman d. shovel

e. tiger

Write the words under the correct categories.

5.

goat	fine	wig
dog	pot	sail
nine	bean	bake

a. **CVC**	b. **CVVC**	c. **CVCV**

Read the sentences. Write the nouns on the lines.

6. a. The rooster crowed. ____________

b. The boy ran. ____________

c. The girl played. ____________

d. The fish swam. ____________

Circle the singular nouns.

7. a. bug bugs b. flags flag

c. maps map d. frog frogs

Circle the plural nouns.

8. a. rivers river b. girl girls

c. bed beds d. nails nail

Circle the common noun.

9. a. Rock River river

b. teacher Mr. Jans

c. Iowa state

d. girl Lisa

Circle the proper noun.

10.

a.	lake	Salt Lake
b.	Denver	city
c.	Ron	boy
d.	Target	store

List three ways that we can communicate.

11. a. ________________________________

b. ________________________________

c. ________________________________

Answer the following question.

12. Why is it important to be a good listener?

____

____

ALTERNATE SPELLING TEST

1	ride	Our dog likes to **ride** in the car.	ride
2	bad	That apple is **bad**.	bad
3	coat	He left his **coat** in the park.	coat
4	went	She **went** for a long walk.	went
5	gave	My mom **gave** me some grapes for a snack.	gave
6	tune	She is whistling a happy **tune**.	tune
7	line	The clothes are hanging on the clothes **line**.	line
8	best	Always try to do your **best** work.	best
9	these	**These** are your toys.	these
10	pail	They used a **pail** to make a sand castle.	pail
11	mean	Our neighbor's dog is **mean**.	mean
12	its	The dog is chasing **its** tail.	its
13	meek	My aunt's horse is **meek** and mild.	meek
14	nice	My grandfather is **nice**.	nice
15	need	The newspapers **need** to be delivered.	need
16	us	Father got **us** a pet hamster.	us
17	green	The grass is **green**.	green
18	sit	Please do not **sit** on that chair.	sit
19	write	He will **write** a letter to his uncle.	write
20	sleep	The dog will **sleep** in the garage.	sleep

LANGUAGE ARTS 202

Unit 2: Action Verbs

TEACHER NOTES

MATERIALS NEEDED FOR LIFEPAC	
Required	Suggested
• sharp pencil	• crayons or colored pencils • notebook or composition book for journaling • paper with guidelines for Spelling Tests

OPTIONAL ADDITIONAL LEARNING ACTIVITIES

This unit is about sports and the importance of following directions. Action verbs are also introduced in this unit. Begin this unit by having the students guess the sport that you are acting out for them. (Some suggestions: baseball—swinging the bat; basketball—dribbling and shooting a basket; soccer—kicking a soccer ball; golf—hitting a golf ball; tennis—swinging a tennis racket, etc.). You may also write various sports on small pieces of paper and students can act out the sport so the other students may guess the sport. Tell the students that this unit will be about different sports and action words.

Section 1

1. Review recognition of vowels by playing a version of "Slap Jack." Use alphabet flashcards as a deck of playing cards. Deal the cards face down evenly to the players. First player lays his top card face up in the middle of the group. The players take turns laying down cards in the middle until a vowel is placed on the pile. Any player may try to slap the pile. The first player to slap the pile gets to take the pile of cards and add them to the bottom of his stack. You can continue to play until someone has all the cards. You may quit after a certain amount of time and the person who has the most cards is the winner.
2. Write these action verbs on small slips of paper:

eat	throw	walk	jump
sleep	dig	smile	sing
laugh	dance	listen	sit

   Put the pieces of paper in a container. Let each student choose a paper, being careful not to let anybody see what is written on the paper. The students have one minute to draw (without talking) the action that is written on the paper they selected. The other students must guess the action verb.

Section 2

1. Following directions activity: Give each student a piece of lined paper. Read the following directions to them:
   a. Write your name on the bottom line of the paper.
   b. Number the top five lines.
   c. Draw a heart on line 2.
   d. Write the name of someone you love on line 3.
   e. Draw a picture of an eye on line 1.
   f. On line 4, copy what was written on lines 1–3.
   g. On line 5, write the words that go with line 4 (see sample).

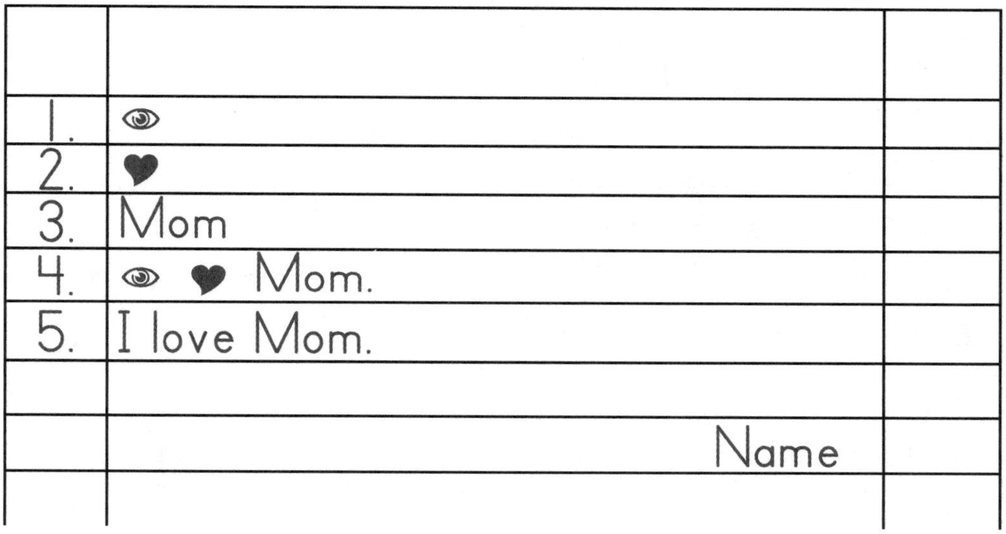

2. Play "Simon Says" (students must listen for the words "Simon says" and follow the directions).
3. Find some comic strips that show a sequence of events that second graders would understand. Cut the strips apart. Let the students put the comic strips in the correct order.

Section 3

1. Give each student an elementary dictionary. Let the students look through the dictionary. First, allow the students to page through the dictionary. Then guide them in finding words. Begin with the word apple. Tell them that the word apple begins with the letter a, so this word will be found at the beginning of the dictionary. Ask them on what page the word apple can be found. Ask the students where they think the word zebra would be found in the dictionary. Tell them to find the word zebra in the dictionary. Ask them on what page zebra is found. Continue having the students find words in the dictionary.
2. Tell the students to find a word in the dictionary that is new to them. Tell the students to tell you (or the rest of the class) the new word. You can guess or have the other students guess the meaning of the word. See who has the closest meaning of the word.

3. Categorizing activity – write these words on slips of paper and place them in a container:

   sports played with a ball
   sports played outside
   things found in a gym
   things found by a swimming pool
   equipment needed to play ice hockey
   equipment needed to play softball
   different kinds of sports balls
   (or any other category you can think of)

   Let the students take turns choosing a slip of paper. Read the paper and tell the students to write as many things that they can think of that go with the subject on the paper. Set a time limit of one and a half minutes to write their lists. Let students read their lists. Each item on the list earns one point for the student. See which student has the most points of all the lists that they made.

4. Choose some Dolch Sight Word flashcards to put in alphabetical order.

Suggested Books:

Play Ball, Amelia Bedelia! by Peggy Parish
Here Comes the Strikeout by Leonard Kessler
Kick, Pass, and Run by Leonard Kessler
The Worst Team Ever by Leonard Kessler
Baseball Ballerina by Kathryn Cristaldi

Journal Suggestions:

1. Guide students to write about their favorite sport. Ask them questions such as:

   What sport do you like to watch?
   What sport do you like to play?
   What skills are needed to play this sport?

   Tell the students to write three or more sentences in their journals about their favorite sports.

2. Write the following on the board or a large piece of paper:

   I must read my Bible and pray
   To help me run the race each day.

   Have the students write this couplet in their journals. Discuss with them the "Race of Life" in which we all are participants.

Administer the LIFEPAC Spelling Test.

Administer the LIFEPAC Test.

ANSWER KEYS

SECTION 1

1.1 See below:

*	f	o	o	t	b	a	l	l	*	*
*	*	*	s	o	c	c	e	r	*	*
*	t	e	n	n	i	s	*	*	*	*
b	a	s	k	e	t	b	a	l	l	*
*	*	p	i	n	g	*	p	o	n	g
*	s	w	i	m	m	i	n	g	*	*
*	*	*	b	a	s	e	b	a	l	l
*	h	o	c	k	e	y	*	*	*	*
v	o	l	l	e	y	b	a	l	l	*
*	*	*	g	o	l	f	*	*	*	*

football, soccer, tennis, basketball, ping pong, swimming, baseball, hockey, volleyball, golf

1.2
a. soccer
b. They make the game fun and fair to all who play.
c. 11 (eleven)
d. protects the goal
e. the goalie

1.3
a. golf
b. hockey
c. soccer
d. tennis
e. baseball
f. football
g. basketball

1.4 Possible answers:
a. always
b. blue
c. hay, key, buy
d. clue
e. due
f. guy
g. buy, hay, key
h. key, hay, buy
i. money
j. monkey
k. played
l. true

1.5
road feet hoe bean blue pie
sheep team due jail tie goat

1.6
a. j**ai**l
b. b**ea**n
c. t**ie**
d. r**oa**d
e. g**oa**t
f. bl**ue**
g. h**oe**
h. sh**ee**p

1.7
a. Jay played in the hay yesterday.
b. The library books are due today.
c. That silly guy wants to buy a blue monkey.
d. Clue and blue are words that sound alike.
e. The man needs money to buy a new key.
f. Is it true that two plus two always equals four?

Teacher check

1.8
a. made
b. cut
c. ran
d. bit
e. smell
f. jumped
g. drew
h. wrote
i. sing
j. sleep
k. gave
l. play

1.9 Teacher check

1.10
- ☑ a. two teams play
- ☐ b. soccer ball used
- ☐ c. hoops and nets used
- ☐ d. peach baskets
- ☐ e. basketball used
- ☑ f. team with the most points wins
- ☐ g. 9 people on a team
- ☑ h. a fun sport to watch and play
- ☐ i. 5 people playing at a time
- ☐ j. used a stick to poke the ball out of the basket

1.11

always	blue
buy	clue
due	guy
hay	key
money	monkey
played	true

1.12 Teacher check

1.13 Any order within categories:

ay words	*uy* words	*ue* words	*ey* words
always	buy	blue	key
hay	guy	clue	money
played		true	monkey
		due	

1.14 Teacher check

1.15
a. walk
b. skip
c. hold
d. sing
e. open
f. buy

1.16 Any order:

store	sidewalk	hands
song	door	store
	cheese	

1.17 Sue, Kay

SELF TEST 1

1.01
a. goat
b. leaf
c. hoe
d. pie
e. blue
f. nail
g. road
h. meet
i. seat

1.02 verb

1.03 noun

1.04
a. noun b. verb
c. verb d. noun
e. noun f. verb

1.05 swam

1.06 splashed

1.07 cried

1.08 hugged

1.09 smiled

SECTION 2

2.1 Possible answers:
a. because
b. chew, stew
c. law, dew
d. fawn
e. flew
f. fraud
g. haul, hawk
h. hawk, haul
i. jaw
j. dew, law
k. pause
l. stew, chew

2.2 Teacher check

2.3 Teacher check

2.4
a. f**au**lt
b. h**au**nt
c. v**au**lt
d. t**au**nt
e. h**au**nch
f. g**au**ze

2.5 Any order:
because, fraud, haul, pause

2.6
a. cl**aw**
b. str**aw**
c. dr**aw**
d. cr**aw**l
e. r**aw**
f. l**aw**n

2.7 Any order:
fawn, hawk, jaw, law

2.8
a. bl**ew**
b. gr**ew**
c. cr**ew**
d. scr**ew**
e. fl**ew**
f. shr**ew**

2.9 Any order:
chew, dew, flew, stew

2.10 See below:

⊠	⊙	f	l	e	w	◈	☺	☺	☺	◈	⊠
⊠	f	r	a	u	d	☺	l	a	w	☺	⊠
⊠	⊙	f	a	w	n	☺	◈	◈	◈	☺	⊠
⊠	⊙	h	a	u	l	☺	j	a	w	☺	⊠
⊠	⊙	c	h	e	w	☺	◈	◈	◈	☺	⊠
⊠	⊙	h	a	w	k	☺	d	e	w	☺	⊠
⊠	⊙	p	a	u	s	e	☺	☺	☺	◈	⊠
b	e	c	a	u	s	e	◈	s	t	e	w

a. i
b. o

2.11 Any order:
flew, fraud, law, fawn, haul, jaw, chew, hawk, dew, pause, because, stew

2.12
a. cake
b. asked
c. bowl
d. turned
e. pan
f. oven
g. baked
h. smell
i. Nick

2.13 Teacher check

2.14
_3_ Tim opened the gift from his parents.
_4_ Tim and his dad played catch.
_1_ It was Tim's birthday. He was eight years old.
_2_ Tim got many presents.

2.15 Teacher check

2.16 Teacher check

2.17 Any order within categories:

Words that sound like foot	Words that sound like tool
brook	goof
book	goose
cookie	boot
nook	moo
good	pool

2.18
a. petunia – a garden plant that has white, pink, and purple flowers
b. phone – a short word meaning telephone
c. photo – a short word meaning photograph

SELF TEST 2

2.01 a. – d. Teacher check
e. 3
f. 8
g. 7
h. 10
i. 00

2.02 Any order:
book, look, wood, hood, took

2.03 Any order:
zoo, room, pool, food, proof

SECTION 3

3.1 Possible answers:
a. cool, cook, wood
b. cook, cool, wood
c. hook, took, food, hood
d. took, hook, food, hood
e. food, took, hook, hood
f. moon, soon
g. pool
h. shook
i. soon, moon
j. hood, hook, took, food
k. wood, cool, cook
l. zoo

3.2 Any order:
cheetah, guppy, lizard, robin

3.3 Any order:
shirt, shoes, gloves, hat

3.4 Any order:
pizza, salad, milk, ice cream

3.5 Any order:
trees, flowers, weeds, grass

3.6 Any order:
Joe, park, slide, Ann, swing, children, dog, faces, ball, Mom, family, home

3.7 Any order:
ran, slid, swung, found, licked, threw, came, walked

3.8 See below:

h	o	c	m	o	o	o	o	c
o	o	w	o	o	d	t	o	o
o	f	o	o	d	o	o	o	o
d	o	o	o	o	o	o	o	l
o	h	s	h	o	o	k	o	o
o	o	o	m	o	c	o	o	k
o	o	o	o	o	o	z	o	o
o	k	o	o	o	p	o	o	l
s	o	o	n	o	o	o	o	o

3.9 Teacher check

3.10 How to Train for a Foot Race:
Eat healthy food.
Wear good shoes.
Get lots of rest.
Run every day.

How to Train for the Race of Life:
Read the Bible.
Obey God and your parents.
Go to church.
Pray to God.

3.11 always, bad, coat, due, egg, fast, gave, hay, its, joke, key, line, money, name, or, pail, queen, ride, sit, trip, under, van, wish, x-ray, yet, zoo

3.12
a. breath – air taken into and sent out of the lungs
b. breathe – when you breathe you take air into your lungs and then send it out
c. brick – a block of clay that is baked hard

3.13 Teacher check

3.14
a. Down: horse
Across: run
b. Down: tiger
Across: eat
c. Down: bunny
Across: jump
d. Down: shark
Across: swim
e. Down: ape
Across: walk
f. Down: lion
Across: growl

3.15 Teacher check

3.16 Teacher check

3.17

Circled words:	Correct spelling:
a. fude	food
b. frawd	fraud
c. plaed	played
d. pauze	pause
e. monee	money
f. zu	zoo
g. cuk	cook
h. lau	law
i. huk	hook
j. troo	true
k. floo	flew
l. gi	guy

SELF TEST 3

3.01 Nouns – any order:
dog, cat, boy, bike, horse, apple, girl, clown

3.02 Verbs – any order:
ran, rode, ate, laughed

3.03 Either order:
softball, soccer

3.04 Either order:
fly, ladybug

3.05 Either order:
books, pencil

3.06 apple

3.07 banana

3.08 carrot

3.09 date

3.010 eggplant

3.011 fig

3.012 grapes

3.013 herbs

UNIT REVIEW

1. Teacher check
Verbs: run, follow, eat, sing, hop, go, carry, ride, find, come
Nouns: monkey, cheese, arm, house, sky, rug, stove, daisy, car, hill

2. meat nail clue beet pie blue
feet soak heat lie pain loan

3. Any order: ea, ee, ai, oa, ue, ie

4.

boot – L	moon – L
good – S	wood – S
cook – S	food – L
cool – L	look – S

5. See below:

b	l	a	w	m	h	a	u	l
u	p	s	t	a	y	g	u	y
y	f	e	w	y	q	v	c	s
s	t	r	a	w	w	k	h	t
x	c	a	u	s	e	e	e	z
d	o	n	k	e	y	y	w	f

6. Categories:
Bugs Kitchen Trees Music

7. b. in ABC order

8.
1. bunny
2. calf
3. duckling
4. foal
5. kitten
6. lamb
7. puppy
8. tadpole

LIFEPAC TEST

1.
a. verb
b. noun
c. verb
d. verb
e. noun

2.

a. nail	a
b. seat	e
c. sheep	e
d. neat	e
e. blue	u
f. lie	i
g. oak	o

3.
a. pl**a**y
b. g**u**y
c. monk**e**y

4.
a. blue
green
purple
red
white
b. Betty
Chad
Jack
Sandy
Will

5.

a. lawn	aw
b. new	ew
c. pause	au

6. Any order within categories:

a.	b.
brook	goof
book	goose
cookie	boot
nook	moo
good	pool

7. e
8. g
9. f
10. a
11. b
12. c
13. d

ALTERNATE LIFEPAC TEST

1. a. flew
b. walked
c. swam
d. drove
e. wrote

2. a. pail – a b. heat – e
c. keep – e d. seat – e
e. glue – u f. tie – i
g. soak – o

3. a. d**<u>a</u>**y b. b**<u>u</u>**y c. donk**<u>e</u>**y

4. bear
goat
panda
ram
whale

5. bee
cricket
moth
spider
wasp

6. aw

7. ew

8. au

9. Any order:
look
hook
cook
crook
hood

10. Any order:
fool
loose
goof
loom
noon

11.

Rules make	the most popular sport in the world.
Reading the Bible	games fun and fair.
Soccer is	protects the goal.
Soccer players	is one way to train for the race of life.
The goalie	cannot touch the soccer ball with their hands.

SPELLING TEST

1	cook	Mother does not want to **cook** tonight.	cook
2	blue	The mountain stream is a beautiful **blue**.	blue
3	key	David lost the **key** to his locker.	key
4	stew	We had beef **stew** for supper.	stew
5	moon	The full **moon** shone brightly over the lake.	moon
6	chew	Remember to **chew** your food with your mouth closed.	chew
7	always	God **always** keeps his promises.	always
8	law	It is important to obey the **law**.	law
9	zoo	The class took a field trip to the **zoo**.	zoo
10	flew	His uncle **flew** a jet.	flew
11	food	We can buy **food** in the grocery store.	food
12	played	Anne **played** the flute in the band.	played
13	jaw	You have an upper and lower **jaw**.	jaw
14	took	Jason **took** the biggest piece of cake.	took
15	true	She read a **true** story about her grandmother.	true
16	fraud	A person is a **fraud** if they are dishonest.	fraud
17	fawn	The doe would not let the **fawn** out of her sight.	fawn
18	shook	They **shook** hands when they met.	shook
19	clue	She wanted a **clue** to the crossword puzzle.	clue
20	cool	The weather is **cool** outside, so please wear a jacket.	cool

LANGUAGE ARTS 202

ALTERNATE LIFEPAC TEST

Name ____________________

Date ____________________

My Score

34/43

Each answer = 1 point

Read the sentences.
Choose the verb that correctly completes each sentence.
Write the word on the line.

1. a. The eagle ____________________ high in the sky.
(flew / walked)

b. The girl ____________________ her pet dog in the park.
(flew / walked)

c. The little fish ________________ away from the big fish.
(drove / swam)

d. Dad ________________ Chris to the swimming pool.
(drove / swam)

e. Jessie ________________ a letter to her grandmother.
(jumped / wrote)

Circle the vowel digraphs in the words.
Write the vowel that does the talking in each word.

2. a. pail ________ b. heat ________

c. keep ________ d. seat ________

e. glue ________ f. tie ________

g. soak ________

Write the vowel *a, e,* or *u* in the blank to correctly spell each word.
Each vowel is used only once.

3. a. d____y b. b____y c. donk____y

Write the words in each category in ABC order.

Animals		**Insects**	
goat	bear	bee	wasp
ram	panda	spider	cricket
whale		moth	

4. ______________________

____

____

____

____

5. ______________________

____

____

____

____

Write the vowel digraphs on the lines next to the words.

6. dawn ________

7. few ________

8. haul ________

Sort the words into the correct categories.

look	hook	goof	cook	hood
fool	loose	loom	crook	noon

Short /o͝o/ as in foot

9. ____________________

____

____

____

____

Long /o͞o/ as in tool

10. ____________________

____

____

____

____

Draw a line from the beginning of each sentence to its correct ending.

11.

Rules make ▸	◂ the most popular sport in the world.
Reading the Bible ▸	◂ games fun and fair.
Soccer is ▸	◂ protects the goal.
Soccer players ▸	◂ is one way to train for the race of life.
The goalie ▸	◂ cannot touch the soccer ball with their hands.

ALTERNATE SPELLING TEST

1	hay	The donkey ate the **hay**.	hay
2	pause	After a **pause** for recess, they went back to class.	pause
3	pool	It was hot so they swam in the **pool**.	pool
4	money	She received **money** for her birthday.	money
5	soon	I hope to get a puppy **soon**!	soon
6	due	That library book is **due** today.	due
7	monkey	My sister wants a pet **monkey**.	monkey
8	guy	The **guy** in the blue uniform is a police officer.	guy
9	dew	There was **dew** on the grass this morning.	dew
10	hood	My new sweatshirt has a **hood**.	hood
11	hawk	The **hawk** has a strong, hooked beak.	hawk
12	wood	The **wood** was too wet to start a campfire.	wood
13	buy	He will **buy** the present with his own money.	buy
14	haul	Trucks **haul** cargo across the country.	haul
15	because	She was dirty **because** she fell in a mud puddle.	because
16	hook	The jacket should hang on the **hook** in the closet.	hook
17	played	My mother **played** the violin in grade school.	played
18	took	She **took** a picture of the baby.	took
19	fawn	The **fawn** was hiding in the tall grass.	fawn
20	always	It is **always** morning somewhere in the world.	always

LANGUAGE ARTS 203

Unit 3: Simple Sentences

TEACHER NOTES

MATERIALS NEEDED FOR LIFEPAC	
Required	Suggested
• sharp pencil	• crayons or colored pencils • notebook or composition book for journaling • paper with guidelines for Spelling Tests

OPTIONAL ADDITIONAL LEARNING ACTIVITIES

This unit is about fables and animal stories. Review with the students the difference between people and animals (this was discussed in Unit 1).

Section 1

1. Share these interesting facts about donkeys after studying the story of Balaam and the donkey:
   - China has the most donkeys in the world—almost 11 million!
   - A male donkey is called a jack. A female donkey is a jenny.
   - Donkeys often live twenty-five years or more.
   - Matthew 21:1-11 tells when Jesus rode a donkey. We celebrate this day as Palm Sunday.
2. Play "Thumbs Up, Thumbs Down." Read the following words. The students are to give you thumbs up if the words are a complete sentence. They should give you a thumbs down if the words are a phrase.

   God made many animals.
   Have soft fur.
   Some animals have feathers.
   There are some animals that live in water.
   The bird in air.
   A cat can be a pet.
   Makes a good pet.
   A dog can be man's best friend.

   Read the phrases again to the students. Discuss with them how to make these phrases into complete sentences.
3. Discuss with students the names of baby animals: bear = cub; cat = kitten; chicken = chick; cow = calf; deer = fawn; dog = puppy; duck = duckling; goat = kid; horse = foal; lion = cub. These and others can be written on cards and used to play a memory game.

Section 2

1. Share these interesting facts about foxes after studying the story of Samson and the foxes.
    - A baby fox is called a kit.
    - There are usually 4-5 kits in a litter.
    - The fox is the smallest member of the dog family.
    - Some foxes can run up to 23 miles per hour!
2. Play a board game or card game together, discussing directions and the importance of knowing and following the directions of a game.
3. Follow a recipe. Cook or bake with your child and show them how important it is to follow the directions found in a recipe.
4. Match animal tracks and the animal.

Section 3

1. Share these interesting facts about hares and tortoises after studying the fable of "The Tortoise and the Hare."
    - A hare is larger than a rabbit.
    - A baby hare is called a kit.
    - A male hare is called a buck.
    - A female hare is called a doe.
    - A tortoise can live to be 100 years old.
    - Tortoises do not have teeth.
    - Some tortoises can weigh as much as 500 pounds.
2. Explore the dictionary with the students. Look for animal pictures in the dictionary.
3. Think about, discuss, or read about Noah and the ark.
4. Read some fables.

Suggested Books:

Animal Fact/Animal Fiction by Seymour Simon
Noah's Ark by Peter Spier
The Classic Treasury of Aesop's Fables by Don Daily
Fables by Arnold Lobel
Look Out for Turtles! by Melvin Berger

Journal Suggestions:

1. Write about pets.
2. Do a mini-study about eagles, referring to this verse: "But they that wait upon the LORD shall renew their strength; they shall mount up with wings as eagles; they shall run, and not be weary; and they shall walk, and not faint" (Isaiah 40:31). Have the students write this verse in their journals.

Songs:

"If I Were a Butterfly" – Words and music by Brian M. Howard

"All Things Bright and Beautiful" – by Cecil Frances Alexander (1818–1895), lyrics based on Genesis 1:31

Administer the LIFEPAC Spelling Test.
The test is provided in this Teacher's Guide.
Evaluate the tests and review the words the students spelled incorrectly.
If necessary, review all of the words in the unit to prepare for the alternate spelling test.
Administer the Alternate LIFEPAC Spelling test that is provided in this Teacher's Guide.

Administer the LIFEPAC Test.
The test is to be administered in one session. Give no help except with directions.
Evaluate the tests and review areas where the students have done poorly.
Review the pages and activities that stress the concepts tested.
If necessary, administer the Alternate LIFEPAC Test.

ANSWER KEYS

SECTION 1

1.1 a. 1
b. 4
c. 2
d. 3
e. 5

1.2 Possible answers:
a. before
b. farm, fern, term, burn
c. fern, farm, term, burn
d. term, farm, fern, burn
e. first
f. park, girl
g. hurt
h. more
i. or
j. girl, park
k. sport
l. burn, farm, fern, term

1.3 a. b**ar**n
b. y**ar**n
c. m**ar**ch
d. h**ar**p
e. b**ar**k
f. p**ar**k
g. p**ar**t
h. **ar**m
i. c**ar**ve

1.4 Any order within categories:
a. **er**: verb, perk, herd, her
b. **ir**: bird, dirt, stir, shirt
c. **ur**: curb, curl, surf, fur

1.5 Teacher check

1.6 Any order:
horse, hawk, lizard, catfish, kangaroo

1.7 Any order:
hop, crawl, gallop, swim, soar

1.8 a. horse – gallop
b. hawk – soar
c. lizard – crawl
d. catfish – swim
e. kangaroo – hop

1.9 cake **N** write **V** look **V** leg **N** jelly **N** see **V**

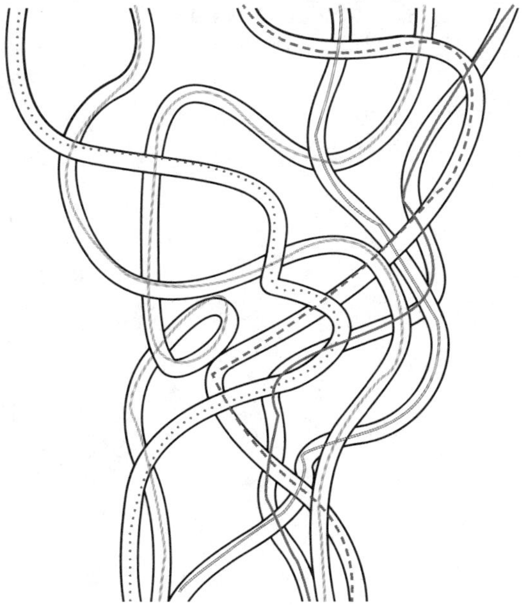

1.10

fern	first
girl	before
or	sport
hurt	burn
farm	more
term	park

1.11 Suggested answers:
a. He would give him a lot of silver and gold.
b. No. He was angry.
c. The donkey saw an angel.
d. He beat the donkey.
e. It talked to Balaam.
f. God made the donkey talk.

1.12 Teacher check

1.13 a. **tr**ophy, **br**occoli, **cr**ib, **pr**incess
b. **cr**ab, **fr**og, **dr**agonfly, **cr**ow
c. **tr**actor, **fr**own, **pr**etzel, **dr**um
d. **cr**ayon, **fr**uit, **br**ead, **tr**umpet
e. **gr**andma, **cr**ate, **gr**apes, **br**ush
f. **tr**ee, **cr**ash, **pr**unes, **br**ick

1.14 Teacher check

1.15 ☒ Plants are green.
☐ Need water and sunshine.
☐ Smell good.
☒ Jessica put the flowers in a vase.
☒ Mother liked the flowers.
☐ Planted more flowers in the garden.

1.16 Suggested answers – answers may vary:
- a. Plants / (need) water and sunshine.
- b. Flowers / (smell) good.
- c. Mother / (planted) more flowers.

1.17
- ☒ Jeff went to the beach.
- ☐ He in the water.
- ☒ The water felt warm on his feet.
- ☐ The dog at the sea gulls.
- ☐ Jeff bubble gum ice cream.
- ☒ He thought the ice cream was good!

1.18
- a. swam
- b. barked
- c. ate

SELF TEST 1

1.01
- a. cart
- b. star
- c. far
- d. jar

1.02 verb, fern, her, term

1.03 girl, bird, dirt

1.04 fur, burn, hurt, curl, purse

1.05 4

1.06 3

1.07 5

1.08 c d f b

1.09
- ☒ Balaam rode on a donkey.
- ☐ Saw an angel.
- ☐ The donkey.
- ☒ The donkey talked to Balaam.
- ☐ Could not see the angel.

1.010
- a. eat
- b. laugh
- c. run
- d. draw

SECTION 2

2.1 a. blade
b. broom
c. close
d. crate
e. drum
f. fry
g. gray
h. plate
i. prize
j. flat
k. glad
l. trail

2.2 Answer: newspapers

2.3
[3] Use the knife to spread some peanut butter on one side of a slice of bread.
[1] Get out two pieces of bread, peanut butter, jelly, a knife, and a plate.
[6] Eat the peanut butter and jelly sandwich.
[4] Then spread jelly on the other slice of bread.
[2] Lay the two pieces of bread on the plate.
[5] Put the two pieces of bread together.

2.4 a. blade
b. broom
c. close
d. crate
e. drum
f. fry
g. gray
h. plate
i. prize
j. flat
k. trail
l. glad

2.5 a. **bl**each b. **bl**ock c. **bl**ess
d. **bl**ow e. **bl**ind f. **bl**ue

2.6 a. **cl**amp b. **cl**ose c. **cl**ear
d. **cl**oud e. **cl**iff f. **cl**own

2.7 a. **fl**ag b. **fl**our c. **fl**ood
d. **fl**ute e. **fl**oor f. **fl**oat

2.8 a. **gl**ee b. **gl**itter c. **gl**obe
d. **gl**ove e. **gl**ide f. **gl**ue

2.9 a. **pl**an b. **pl**ate c. **pl**ow
d. **pl**anet e. **pl**ay f. **pl**ant
g. **pl**uck h. **pl**ease i. **pl**us

2.10 a. **sl**am b. **sl**eep c. **sl**ime
d. **sl**ap e. **sl**eeve f. **sl**ip
g. **sl**ant h. **sl**ide i. **sl**ow

2.11 Teacher check

2.12 Teacher check – circled words:
a. ran
b. slid
c. swung
d. found
e. licked
f. threw
g. came
h. walked

2.13 a. Sam
b. The nest
c. The mother bird
d. Three baby birds

2.14 a. rode
b. floated
c. touched
d. flew
e. liked
f. told

2.15 a. Josh / rode in a hot air balloon.
b. The balloon / floated above the trees.
c. Josh / touched the leaves.
d. A bird / flew by the balloon.
e. Josh / liked the balloon ride.
f. He / told his friends about it.

2.16 a. made the world
b. The Bible
c. Jesus

2.17 Teacher check

2.18 a. strong
b. Philistines
c. 300
d. tails
e. torch
f. burned
g. God

2.19 See below:

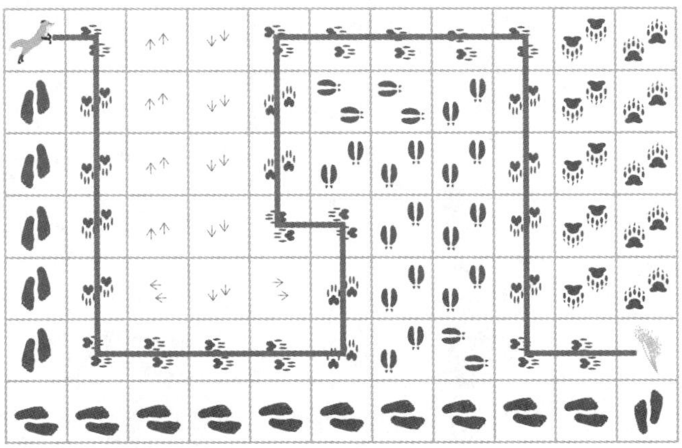

2.20 Teacher check

2.21 Either order:
a. raft, lift
b. jump, limp
c. wild, told
d. band, pond
e. last, nest
f. bank, junk
g. want, hint
h. desk, mask

2.22
a. jump
b. bank
c. junk
d. desk
e. lift
f. nest

2.23 Teacher check

e(d)ge	1. eat
e(a)t	2. ebony
e(g)g	3. echo
e(f)fort	4. edge
e(e)l	5. eel
e(b)ony	6. effort
e(c)ho	7. egg

2.24 Teacher check

2.25
1. ape
2. bison
3. cat
4. cow
5. deer
6. dog
7. giraffe
8. kangaroo
9. penguin
10. sheep
11. yak
12. zebra

SELF TEST 2

2.01 b.

2.02 Any order:
bike, dog, boat, flower, pizza

2.03 Any order:
ate, growl, rode, smell, swam

2.04	a. bl	**bl**ow
	b. cl	**cl**oud
2.05	a. gl	**gl**ide
	b. fl	**fl**ag
2.06	a. sl	**sl**ip
	b. pl	**pl**us
2.07	a. ld	wi**ld**
	b. ft	li**ft**
2.08	a. mp	da**mp**
	b. nd	sa**nd**
2.09	a. nk	ju**nk**
	b. nt	wa**nt**
2.010	a. st	ne**st**
	b. sk	a**sk**

2.011 Angela

2.012 bike

2.013 skated

2.014 barked

2.015
1. book
2. eraser
3. map
4. paper
5. pencil
6. ruler

2.016 complete

2.017 subject

2.018 noun

2.019 verb

2.020 phrase

SECTION 3

3.1 Possible Answers:
a. ant
b. list, land, desk
c. junk
d. left, hold
e. gift
f. land, list, desk
g. hold, left
h. desk, list, land
i. lump
j. wind, most
k. ramp
l. most, wind

3.2
a. I see a gorilla.
b. The gorilla ate a banana.
c. The gorilla ran to the tree.
d. It climbed up the tree.
e. We laughed at the gorilla.

3.3
a. see
b. ate
c. ran
d. climbed
e. laughed

3.4 Circled words: I, gorilla, gorilla, It, We

3.5
a. h**o**ld
b. l**a**nd
c. w**i**nd
d. j**u**nk
e. d**e**sk
f. g**i**ft
g. r**a**mp
h. l**u**mp
i. l**e**ft
j. **a**nt
k. l**i**st
l. m**o**st

3.6
[5] The tortoise won the race.
[3] The hare quickly began the race.
[1] The hare won many animal races.
[2] The tortoise asked the hare to race him.
[4] The hare took a nap under a shade tree.

3.7
a. ant
b. desk
c. gift
d. hold
e. junk
f. land
g. left
h. list
i. lump
j. most
k. ramp
l. wind

3.8 Teacher check
1. ant
2. desk
3. gift
4. hold
5. junk
6. land
7. left
8. list
9. lump
10. most
11. ramp
12. wind

3.9 Teacher check

3.10 Suggested answers:
a. The cat found a toy.
b. The cat forgot about the mouse.

3.11 Suggested answers – answers may vary:
a. Kyle (*or* He) made lunch.
b. He made a ham sandwich.
c. He put cheese on his sandwich.
d. He made a sandwich for his sister.
e. They ate the sandwiches in the kitchen.
f. He made two sandwiches.

3.12 Teacher check

3.13
a. farm
b. left
c. park
d. gift
e. fern
f. drum
g. hold
h. term
i. ramp
j. first
k. gray
l. lump
m. girl
n. land
o. wind
p. junk
q. ant
r. sport
s. desk
t. burn
u. list
v. hurt
w. flat
x. most
y. or

SELF TEST 3

3.01 Sara went swimming.
3.02 The water was cold.
3.03 The sunshine felt warm.
3.04 Sara liked the warm sunshine.
3.05 i(l)l   i(c)e   i(f)   i(g)l o o   i(n)   i(d)o l
1. ice   4. igloo
2. idol   5. ill
3. if   6. in

3.06
a. ☒ Jeff went to the beach.
b. ☐ He in the water.
c. ☒ The water felt warm on his feet.
d. ☐ The dog at the sea gulls.
e. ☐ Jeff bubble gum ice cream.
f. ☒ He thought the ice cream was good!

3.07 predicate
3.08 noun
3.09 verb
3.010 phrase
3.011 hare
3.012 tortoise
3.013 hare
3.014 tortoise

UNIT REVIEW

1. arm
2. her
3. sir
4. burn
5. Any order:
fox, lake, tree, hare
6. Any order:
run, eat, laugh, sleep
7. (Ann) <u>rode</u> her (bike).
8. (Flowers) <u>smell</u> good.
9. (Ben) <u>saw</u> a (cat).
10. The (cat) <u>chased</u> a (mouse).
11. Answer: tree

LIFEPAC TEST

1. Teacher check
2. 7
3. 3
4. 5
5. 5
6. a. **c**rib b. **t**rot
c. **p**rint d. **g**rin
7. d
8. create (egg) (jacket) write tell
(nose) sit (peach) (cake) wear
9. Samson was a strong man.
10. a. Balaam
b. donkey
11. a. rode
b. talked
12. Suggested answers:
a. The mouse found some cheese.
b. The cat chased the mouse.
c. The cat ate the cheese.
13. a. ra(ft) b. go(ld)
c. la(mp) d. wi(nd)
e. si(nk) f. a(nt)
g. de(sk) h. fa(st)

ALTERNATE LIFEPAC TEST

1. a – d Teacher check
2. 3
3. 7
4. 5
5. 5
6. a. **b**ring
b. **t**rot
c. **d**raw
d. **f**resh
7. Balaam rode on a donkey.
8. a. hare
b. tortoise
9. a. ran
b. won
10. a
11. Nouns – any order:
chin
hen
shoes
apple
cookie
12. Verbs – any order:
make
flew
eat
rode
run
13. Suggested answer:
Grandmother made sugar cookies.
14. Suggested answer:
Allie helped Grandmother.
15. Suggested answer:
Allie and Grandmother ate three cookies.
16. a. so(ft) b. co(ld)
c. ca(mp) d. e(nd)
e. du(nk) f. se(nt)
g. a(sk) h. fir(st)
17. Answer: a comb
18. a, e, i, o, u
19. park
20. crate
21. fry
22. before

SPELLING TEST			
1	left	Ted writes with his **left** hand.	left
2	gray	The **gray** kitten is my favorite.	gray
3	hurt	The cowboy **hurt** his arm.	hurt
4	ant	The **ant** is a hardworking insect.	ant
5	flat	That car has a **flat** tire.	flat
6	sport	Football is a popular **sport** in the U.S.	sport
7	gift	The **gift** was wrapped in pretty paper.	gift
8	crate	Grandma bought a **crate** of peaches.	crate
9	park	We had a picnic in the **park**.	park
10	wind	The **wind** blew the sailboat across the lake.	wind
11	drum	He pounded the **drum** loudly.	drum
12	first	She was **first** in line to go down the slide.	first
13	desk	The book is on the **desk**.	desk
14	close	Don't forget to **close** the door when you come in!	close
15	fern	There is a **fern** growing in the garden.	fern
16	junk	That **junk** belongs in the garbage.	junk
17	prize	She won first **prize** in the spelling bee.	prize
18	farm	They like living on a **farm**.	farm
19	list	There are twelve words in our spelling **list**.	list
20	glad	Are you **glad** that you are now finished with your test?	glad

LANGUAGE ARTS 203

ALTERNATE LIFEPAC TEST

Name ____________________

Date ____________________

Each answer = 1 point

Follow these directions and answer the questions.

1.
   a. Color **green** the words with the letters **ar** as in **är**.
   b. Color **red** the words with the letters **er** as in **ûr**.
   c. Color **purple** the words with the letters **ir** as in **ûr**.
   d. Color **blue** the words with the letters **ur** as in **ûr**.

art	first	germ	tar	stir
part	skirt	fern	firm	verb
nerve	term	jerk	turn	surf
curl	thirst	burp	burn	herd

2. How many words are colored green? ____________

3. How many words are colored red? ____________

4. How many words are colored blue? ____________

5. How many words are colored purple? ____________

The letters *br, cr, dr, fr, gr, pr,* and *tr* are consonant blends.
Add the letters *b, f, d,* or *t* to the blanks to make a word.

6. a. ___ ring b. ____ rot c. ___ raw d. __ resh

Circle the group of words that is a complete sentence.

7. Balaam rode on a donkey.

Was a strong man.

The hare.

Circle the subject in each sentence.

8. a. The hare ran fast.
b. The tortoise won the race.

Underline the action verb in each sentence.

9. a. The hare ran fast.
b. The tortoise won the race.

Circle the group of words that is in the correct ABC order.

10.

a.	b.	c.	d.
aster	aster	aster	aster
daffodil	daisy	daffodil	daffodil
daisy	daffodil	daisy	daisy
lilac	lilac	rose	lilac
rose	rose	lilac	violet
tulip	tulip	violet	tulip
violet	violet	tulip	rose

Sort the words into the correct categories.

make	**hen**	**shoes**	**eat**	**road**
chin	**flew**	**apple**	**cookie**	**run**

Nouns	**Verbs**
11. ____________________	**12.** ____________________
____________________	____________________
____________________	____________________
____________________	____________________
____________________	____________________

Read the story.
Answer the questions about the story using complete sentences.
You may use sentences from the story in your answer.

Cookies with Grandmother

Grandmother made sugar cookies. Allie helped Grandmother. She put the cookie dough on the pan. Grandmother put the pan in the oven. The cookies smelled good! Allie and Grandmother ate three cookies!

13. What kind of cookies did Grandmother make?

____

____

14. Who helped Grandmother?

____

____

15. How many cookies did Allie and Grandmother eat?

____

____

Circle the ending consonant blends in the words.

16.

a. soft	b. cold
c. camp	d. end
e. dunk	f. sent
g. ask	h. first

Read the directions and solve the riddle.

What has teeth but doesn't eat?

a. Write the letter **b** on the last line.

b. On the third line, write the letter **o**.

c. Write the letter **a** on line one.

d. Write the letter **m** on line four.

e. On line two, write the letter **c**.

17. ________ ________ ________ ________ ________

1. 2. 3. 4. 5.

Circle the five vowels in the alphabet.

18.

a b c d e f g h i j k l m n o p q r s t u v w x y z

Write the correct spelling of the misspelled words.

19. parke ____________________

20. kraet ____________________

21. fri ____________________

22. befour ____________________

ALTERNATE SPELLING TEST

1	girl	The **girl** rode her bike on the sidewalk.	girl
2	broom	Mother swept the kitchen floor with a **broom**.	broom
3	term	The president is in his first **term** in office.	term
4	ramp	There is a new skateboard **ramp** at the park.	ramp
5	fry	It is so hot you can **fry** an egg on the sidewalk.	fry
6	before	The letter *a* comes **before** the letter *b* in the alphabet.	before
7	hold	Please **hold** my hand while we cross the street.	hold
8	trail	There were several people on the nature **trail**.	trail
9	more	Six is **more** than two.	more
10	lump	I found a large **lump** in my oatmeal.	lump
11	blade	There is a **blade** of grass on my shoe.	blade
12	or	Would you like chocolate **or** vanilla ice cream?	or
13	most	She has the **most** stuffed animals I ever saw!	most
14	plate	Grandmother brought us a **plate** of brownies.	plate
15	burn	Do not **burn** your hand on the stove.	burn
16	land	The farmer bought some more **land**.	land
17	park	Nate will **park** his bike in the garage.	park
18	desk	The teacher has a large **desk**.	desk
19	gray	My grandfather has **gray** hair.	gray
20	hurt	It would **hurt** to fall off a swing.	hurt

LANGUAGE ARTS 204

Unit 4: Types of Sentences

TEACHER NOTES

MATERIALS NEEDED FOR LIFEPAC	
Required	Suggested
• sharp pencil	• crayons or colored pencils • notebook or composition book for journaling • paper with guidelines for Spelling Tests

OPTIONAL ADDITIONAL LEARNING ACTIVITIES

This unit is about special days, holidays, and celebrations. Introduce this unit by reading Ecclesiastes 3:1 – "To every thing there is a season, and a time to every purpose under heaven." God gave us special days to celebrate. The people in the Bible celebrated special days. In this unit, we will be studying special days called holidays. Reading the book *A Time to Keep: The Tasha Tudor Book of Holidays* by Tasha Tudor would be a good introduction to this unit.

Section 1

1. Review the sounds of *sh*, *ch*, and *wh* with the students. Read the words in the list. Tell the students to listen to the beginning sound of each word. If they hear the sh sound, they are to put their pointer finger up to their closed mouth (representing the *sh* or quiet sign). If they hear the *ch* sound they are to flap their wings like a chicken. If they hear the *wh* sound, they are to show three fingers (like the letter *w*).

child	she	white
what	chair	sheep
shout	when	cheer

2. Share with the students some of the traditions or yearly activities that you observe at Christmas. Read a book about different Christmas customs from around the world (see the Suggested Reading List for ideas). Discuss the different customs with the children.

3. Read these sentences to the students. If the sentence is a statement sentence and should end with a period, the students should put a hand to their head. If the sentence is a question sentence and should end with a question mark, the students should fold their hands. If the sentence is an exclamation sentence and should end with an exclamation mark, the students should raise their hand.

   Wow! It is sure quiet in here!
   Are you being a good listener?
   It is important to be a good listener.

Section 2

1. Look at a calendar with the students. Point out that the months of the year, days of the week, and special days or holidays (if listed on the calendar) are proper nouns that begin with a capital letter.
2. Ask the students these questions. Have them say the answer to you in a complete sentence.

   What did you have for breakfast this morning?
   Is the sun shining today?
   Is it warm or cool outside?
   What color is the shirt you are wearing?
   Where did you eat supper last night?
   Who is in the room with you?
   When is it time to go to bed?
   How are you answering these questions?

Section 3

1. Read this story, "Birthday Boy," to the students. Ask some comprehension questions.

Birthday Boy

Sam rolled out of bed. He yawned and stretched bigger than ever.

"Breakfast is ready!" yelled his mom.

Sam threw on some jeans. He put on his favorite red baseball shirt. He ran down the stairs. There, on the table, was his birthday breakfast.

On April 10, for the last 7 years, Sam's mom made him a birthday breakfast. It was a large waffle with strawberries on top and a chocolate milkshake with whipped cream and a cherry. It was the best breakfast Sam could ever ask for. And he only got it once a year.

"Eat your breakfast, Sam. Your dad will be in the house soon. We'll give you your present when he comes in," said Mom.

Sam started to eat a little quicker. I wonder what they got me this year, he thought to himself. Stomp, stomp, stomp! His dad was coming! Sam quickly ate the last bite of his waffle. He drank the last bit of his milkshake and looked towards the doorway.

"Happy Birthday, Bud!" said his dad. He rubbed the top of Sam's head.

"Thanks, Dad," Sam said.

Dad placed a colorful box in front of him. Sam tore open the wrapping paper. He ripped open the box. Inside was a brand new baseball glove. It was the one that he saw in the store.

"Awesome!" yelled Sam. "Want to go outside and play catch, Dad?"

"Sure, Sam, let's go!"

Suggested Books:

Children Just Like Me—Celebrations! by Barnabas and Anabel Kindersley
Richard Scarry's Best Times Ever: A Book About Seasons and Holidays by Richard Scarry
A Tree for All Seasons: A National Geographic Book by Robin Bernard
Christmas around the World by Mary D. Lankford
Christmas around the World by Emily Kelley

Journal Suggestions:

1. Write in their journal about what the date is of their birthday. They may write about a special birthday gift, or the cake they like, etc.
2. Write the Genesis 8:22 or Daniel 1:21a on the board or a large piece of paper:

   While the earth remaineth, seedtime and harvest, and cold and heat, and summer and winter, and day and night shall not cease. Genesis 8:22

   And he changeth the times and seasons... Daniel 2:21a

   Have the students write one of these verses in their journals. Talk about the four seasons with the students. Tell the students to illustrate the verse with drawings of the four seasons.

Administer the LIFEPAC Spelling Test.
The test is provided in this Teacher's Guide.
Evaluate the tests and review the words the students spelled incorrectly.
If necessary, review all of the words in the unit to prepare for the alternate spelling test.
Administer the Alternate LIFEPAC Spelling test that is provided in this Teacher's Guide.

Administer the LIFEPAC Test.
The test is to be administered in one session. Give no help except with directions.
Evaluate the tests and review areas where the students have done poorly.
Review the pages and activities that stress the concepts tested.
If necessary, administer the Alternate LIFEPAC Test.

ANSWER KEYS

SECTION 1

1.1 Christmas

Easter

Valentine's Day

Thanksgiving

President's Day

Independence Day

1.2 Possible answers:
- a. chain, shame, chess
- b. their, those
- c. chat
- d. thin
- e. chess, chain, shame
- f. third
- g. quit
- h. those, their
- i. shame, chain, chess
- j. whale
- k. sheep
- l. wheel

1.3
- a. **sh**ack b. **sh**ed
- c. **sh**ip d. **sh**op
- e. **sh**ut f. ca**sh**
- g. fre**sh** h. fi**sh**
- i. slo**sh** j. ru**sh**

1.4
- a. **ch**at b. **ch**ess
- c. **ch**ick d. **ch**op
- e. **ch**um f. ar**ch**
- g. ea**ch** h. ri**ch**
- i. ou**ch** j. mu**ch**

1.5
- a. **wh**ale b. **wh**eel
- c. **wh**ip d. **wh**oa
- e. **wh**y

1.6
- a. chick
- b. whale
- c. rich
- d. fish
- e. chat
- f. wheel
- g. ship
- h. whoa
- i. shop

1.7 Teacher check

1.8 Circled items:
- a. Have ?
- b. Jake .
- c. What ?
- d. They .
- e. Jake .
- f. Are ?
- g. Karen .
- h. She .
- i. Some .
- j. Did ?
- k. Karen .
- l. They .

1.9
- a. wheel
- b. chain
- c. those
- d. sheep
- e. third
- f. whale
- g. chat
- h. their
- i. shame
- j. chess
- k. thin
- l. quit

1.10 Answer: in case he had a hole-in-one

1.11 Suggested answers – answers may vary:
- a. They made Christmas cookies.
- b. She liked the angel cookie cutter.
- c. They read a book.
- d. She used pink frosting.
- e. Student answer

1.12 Teacher check

1.13 Teacher check

1.14 a. **qu**ail b. **qu**ake
c. **qu**een d. **qu**it
e. **qu**ote f. **qu**iz

1.15 a. ba**ck** b. de**ck**
c. du**ck** d. ki**ck**
e. li**ck** f. lo**ck**
g. mo**ck** h. ne**ck**
i. pa**ck** j. pi**ck**
k. ra**ck** l. sa**ck**
m. si**ck** n. so**ck**
o. ti**ck** p. to**ck**
q. tu**ck** r. yu**ck**

1.16

a. **qu**iz	little or no sound
b. **qu**ack	fast, speedy
c. **qu**ake	a short test
d. **qu**arrel	a sound that a duck makes
e. **qu**arter	to fight with words
f. **qu**een	to stop doing something
g. **qu**ick	to shake or tremble
h. **qu**iet	a wife of a king
i. **qu**ilt	a soft blanket or covering
j. **qu**it	25 cents

1.17 The Clock Trick
Cherry Chicken and Donna Duck were pecking away in the muck looking for a snack of black ticks to smack on.
"Cluck," said Cherry when she found something good to eat.
"Quack," said Donna when she found something good to eat.
The rest of the birds in the flock wanted to play a trick on the chicken and the duck. They stuck a clock in the muck. The tick-tock sound made Cherry and Donna crazy. They wanted to stop the tick-tock. They pecked at the clock in the muck. It did not stop. They gave it a whack with a stick. It did not stop. They kicked a rock at it. It did not stop. They took it to Peter Peacock. He stuck the clock in a sack and threw it in a pick-up truck. Farmer Jack drove off with the clock in the truck. The clock never came back.

1.18 Teacher check

1.19 Teacher check

1.20 a. ?
b. !
c. .
d. .
e. !
f. .
g. ?
h. !, ! *or* .

SELF TEST 1

1.01 Christmas
1.02 Thanksgiving
1.03 **wh**en
1.04 **sh**ot
1.05 **ch**ess
1.06 **qu**it
1.07 pi**ck**
1.08 **qu**een
1.09 a. !, ! *or* .
b. !
c. .
d. .
e. .
f. ?
g. .

1.010

Kristy and her mom made	Kristy's favorite cookie cutter.
The angel was	on the angel cookie.
Mom and Kristy read	Christmas cookies.
	a book while the cookies baked.
Kristy put pink frosting	

SECTION 2

2.1 Possible answers:
- a. children
- b. share
- c. this, then
- d. short, shark
- e. quail, quiet
- f. chip
- g. then, this
- h. white, while
- i. shark, short
- j. quiet, quail
- k. while, white
- l. why

2.2 See below:

1. I	sleep	can	me
2. puzzle	read	~~pencil~~	run
3. she	circle	and	write
4. paper	talk	~~he~~	follow
5. book	~~story~~	talk	directions

2.3 Answer: I can read and follow directions.

2.4 Teacher check

2.5
- a. then — b. share
- c. children — d. quail
- e. why — f. chip
- g. short — h. white
- i. shark — j. this
- k. while — l. quiet

2.6
- a. Mess Hall
- b. tree
- c. Little
- d. rabbit *or* bunny
- e. Lazy
- f. Tiny
- g. fire pit
- h. Riding Stables

2.7 Any order within categories:

Hard *th*		Soft *th*	
that	this	thaw	think
they	there	thud	thing
them	these	thick	third

2.8
Sunday
Monday
Tuesday
Wednesday
Thursday
Friday
Saturday

2.9
- a. ray, april, and i went on vacation.
  Ray, April, I
- b. we went to denver, colorado.
  We, Denver, Colorado
- c. april wanted to hike in the rocky mountains.
  April, Rocky, Mountains
- d. ray and i went to the grocery store on oak street.
  Ray, I, Oak, Street
- e. i saw ray buy a pepsi.
  I, Ray, Pepsi
- f. he gave the pepsi to april.
  He, Pepsi, April

2.10
- ☐ Jeff told me that he is going to the park.
- ☒ i wanted to go to the park with Jeff.
- ☒ mom said that i could ride my bike.
- ☐ Dad told me to be careful when I crossed the street.
- ☐ I am glad that I can go to the park with Jeff.
- ☒ Jeff and i are good friends.

2.11 Suggested answers – answers may vary.
- a. They were going to celebrate the Fourth of July.
- b. They ate breakfast.
- c. They wanted to play goofy golf.
- d. The children would get lots of candy from the parade.
- e. It was finally the Fourth of July!
  Yes, this was an exciting day for Rachel and Neal!

2.12 Teacher check

2.13

ba**ng**	fa**ng**	lu**ng**	ri**ng**
so**ng**	stri**ng**	thi**ng**	su**ng**
ha**ng**	di**ng**	sa**ng**	ki**ng**

2.14 Teacher check

SELF TEST 2

2.01 a. – f. Teacher check
Answer: your nose
2.02 thanksgiving
2.03 thursday
2.04 mom, sam
2.05 i
2.06 the
2.07 Any order within categories:
thaw, thick, thing, think, third, thud
2.08 Any order within categories:
that, them, there, these, they, this
2.09 the
2.010 them
2.011 there
2.012 They
2.013 ring
2.014 sing
2.015 string
2.016 bring

SECTION 3

3.1 Possible answers:
a. both
b. fish, dish
c. dish, fish
d. math
e. rich, neck, rock, sack, rush, wash
f. path
g. neck, rich, rock, sack, rush, wash
h. rock, rich neck, sack, rush, wash
i. sack, rich, neck, rock, rush, wash
j. rush, rich, neck, rock, sack, wash
k. wash, rich, neck, rock, sack, rush
l. which

3.2

Betsy	help her run fast.
The wind	runs with Betsy.
Her new	likes to run.
tennis shoes	blows through
The dog	her hair.

3.3 a. Betsy likes to run.
b. The wind blows through her hair.
c. Her new tennis shoes help her run fast.
d. The dog runs with Betsy.
Teacher check
3.4 Teacher check
3.5 a. both b. dish
c. fish d. math
e. neck f. path
g. rich h. rock
i. rush j. sack
k. wash l. which
3.6 See below:

i	n	f	o	r	m	a	t	i	o	n	x	z	b
y	m	a	g	a	z	i	n	e	r	e	a	d	o
x	e	n	c	y	c	l	o	p	e	d	i	a	o
z	v	w	d	i	c	t	i	o	n	a	r	y	k
n	e	w	s	p	a	p	e	r	q	m	a	p	s
w	l	i	b	r	a	r	y	w	o	r	d	s	v

3.7 Any order:
bean, bee, beast, bear
3.8 Any order:
frost, fruit, froze, frog
3.9 Any order:
mollusk, moist, mole, mommy

3.10 Any order:
ride, rig, ring, right

3.11 Any order:
take, tag, tall, tale

3.12 Teacher check

3.13 Teacher check

3.14

a.	chidlren	children
b.	wich	which
c.	ches	chess
d.	shaim	shame
e.	washe	wash
f.	thier	their
g.	wile	while
h.	thoes	those
i.	mathe	math
j.	whail	whale
k.	sak	sack
l.	ritch	rich

3.15 Teacher check

SELF TEST 3

3.01

Dan	pass the ball to each other
Greg and Dan	bounces high off the floor
The basketball	likes to play basketball

a. Dan likes to play basketball
b. Greg and Dan pass the ball to each other.
c. The basketball bounces high off the floor.

3.02 Any order:
donkey, dove, dolphin

3.03 Any order:
goat, goldfish, guppy

3.04 Any order:
skunk, snake, snail

3.05 Suggested answer:
The sky is blue.

3.06 Suggested answer:
A dog has four legs.

3.07 Suggested answer:
The birthday of Jesus is at Christmas time.

3.08 ring

3.09 bang

3.010 lung

UNIT REVIEW

1. Thanksgiving
2. Memorial Day
3. Christmas
4. Independence Day
5. ?
6. .
7. ! *or* .
8. ?
9. Suggested answer:
   Yes, I like to read.
10. Suggested answer:
    Yes, I like to go to the library.
11. **wh**eel
12. **sh**ut
13. **ch**ess
14. **ch**ip (*or* **sh**ip, **wh**ip)
15. **wh**ip (*or* **ch**ip, **sh**ip)
16. **sh**ip (*or* **ch**ip, **wh**ip)
17. ~~that~~
18. (think)
19. ~~they~~
20. (thaw)
21. ~~them~~
22. (thing)
23. stri**ng**
24. si**ng**
25. ki**ng**
26. sti**ng**
27. Karen went to the beach.
28. She asked me to go along.
29. I told Karen that I could not go with her.
30. She took her friend Sara to the beach.
31. Either order: bean, bear
32. Either order: frog, froze
33. Either order: mold, mole

LIFEPAC TEST

1. .
2. ?
3. .
4. ?
5. .
6. What will (rex) do on the ranch?
7. (rex) will ride on a horse.
8. (what) is the name of the horse?
9. The horse's name is (ginger).
10. Uncle Dan will ride a horse named (cole).
11. Q
12. S
13. Q
14. S
15. a. **sh**ip b. **wh**ale c. **sh**ark
    d. **ch**ick e. **wh**istle f. **ch**ess
16. a. (qu)een b. du(ck) c. (th)em d. so(ng)
    e. ma(th) f. ba(ng) g. (qu)iet h. ba(ck)
17. b
18. c
19. a
20. January
21. Friday
22. May
23. I
24. June
25. a. ~~there~~ b. (thing)
    c. ~~that~~ d. ~~they~~
    e. ~~them~~ f. (think)

ALTERNATE LIFEPAC TEST

1. a. ?
b. .
c. .
d. ?
e. .

2. a. What will linda do on the farm?
b. linda will help Grandma.
c. grandma and Linda will plant a garden.
d. fido and Spot are Grandma's dogs.

3. a. S
b. Q
c. Q
d. S

4. **wh**eel
5. **wh**ale
6. **sh**eep
7. **ch**ild
8. **ch**ain
9. **sh**oe

10. a. deck b. sing
c. quail d. there
e. king f. luck
g. thin h. quake

11. a. subject
b. verb
c. subject
d. verb

12. a. dove
b. giggle
c. one

13. b
14. a
15. c
16. a

17. a. Friday
b. Christmas
c. April
d. Denver
e. Thanksgiving

18. a. – e. Teacher check
Answer: a bat

SPELLING TEST

1	wash	Remember to **wash** your hands before you eat.	wash
2	shark	They saw a **shark** in the ocean.	shark
3	third	This is the **third** word in the spelling test.	third
4	math	**Math** is John's favorite subject.	math
5	quiet	It was so **quiet** that you could hear a pin drop.	quiet
6	chess	The game of **chess** is a game of strategy.	chess
7	fish	Ella got a **fish** for her aquarium.	fish
8	white	The **white** snow glittered brightly.	white
9	whale	The fishermen were frightened by the large **whale**.	whale
10	path	Jenny rode on the bike **path**.	path
11	quail	The **quail** ran across the road.	quail
12	wheel	Jacob's bicycle has a broken **wheel**.	wheel
13	sack	The groceries were put in a **sack**.	sack
14	share	The sisters will **share** a bedroom.	share
15	sheep	The **sheep** are in the pasture.	sheep
16	rock	The mother likes to **rock** her baby.	rock
17	children	The **children** were excited for the birthday party.	children
18	shame	Her lie made her blush with **shame**.	shame
19	rich	Many thought Frank was **rich**.	rich
20	why	My little sister's favorite word is "**why**."	why

LANGUAGE ARTS 204

ALTERNATE LIFEPAC TEST

Name ____________________

Date ____________________

My Score

38 / 47

Each answer = 1 point

Read the sentences.
Put the correct punctuation at the end of each sentence.

1.
   a. Why is Linda happy___
   b. Linda is very happy___
   c. Linda will go to visit her Grandma Scott___
   d. Where does Grandma Scott live___
   e. Grandma lives on a farm___

Read the sentences. Some words needs capital letters.
Circle the words that need capital letters.

2.
   a. What will linda do on the farm?
   b. linda will help Grandma.
   c. grandma and Linda will plant a garden.
   d. fido and Spot are Grandma's dogs.

Read the sentences.
If the sentence makes a statement, write the letter *S* on the blank.
If the sentence asks a question, write a Q on the blank.

3. a. It is Shane's birthday. ________

b. How old is Shane? ________

c. Are there eight candles on the birthday cake? ________

d. Shane is eight years old. ________

Add the consonant blend *sh*, *ch*, or *wh* to the blanks to complete each word. The pictures will give you a hint.

4. ___ ___eel **5.** ___ ___ale **6.** ___ ___eep

7. ___ ___ild **8.** ___ ___ain **9.** ___ ___oe

Read the words. Circle the consonant blends in each word.

10. a. deck b. sing c. quail d. there

e. king f. luck g. thin h. quake

Read the sentences.
Identify the underlined word as either a subject or a verb.
Write *subject* or *verb* on the line after each sentence.

11. a. Babies are little. ____________

b. Babies sleep a lot. ____________

c. Mike has a new baby brother. ____________

d. Mike smiles at his baby brother. ____________

Read the words below.
Write each word next to the correct guide words.

one	giggle	dove

12. a. donkey • dragon ____________

b. germ • glass ____________

c. of • open ____________

Read the questions.
Circle the letter of each answer that is a complete sentence.

13. What color is the sky?

a. Is blue.

b. The sky is blue.

c. The sky.

14. Who is God's son?

a. Jesus is God's son.

b. Jesus.

c. Jesus God's son.

15. How old are you?

a. Eight years old.

b. Eight.

c. I am eight years old.

16. Who made the earth?

a. God made the earth.

b. God.

c. Made the earth.

Read the words.
Circle the word in each row that is correctly capitalized.

17.

a.	Friday	october	fred
b.	snake river	Christmas	sunday
c.	April	i	fourth of July
d.	joe	march	Denver
e.	Thanksgiving	friday	fluffy

Follow the directions to find the mystery words.

The mystery words will answer this question:

What animal is best at hitting a baseball?

a. Write an X on the third letter of the alphabet.

b. Draw a triangle (△) around the last letter of the alphabet.

c. Put a circle (○) around the vowels.

d. Put a box (□) around the letters **b** and **t**.

e. Write the letters that have a **circle** or a **box** around them on the lines below.

a	**c**	**c**	**c**	**z**	**z**	**c**
z	**z**	**b**	**z**	**z**	**c**	**a**
z	**z**	**c**	**c**	**t**	**z**	**z**

18. __________ __________ __________ __________

ALTERNATE SPELLING TEST

1	thin	The smoke vanished into **thin** air.	thin
2	rush	They had to **rush** because they were late.	rush
3	short	Betsy had a **short** stack of pancakes for breakfast.	short
4	quit	They had to **quit** the ball game because it began to rain.	quit
5	which	Jason had to decide **which** present to open first.	which
6	chip	Most children like chocolate **chip** cookies.	chip
7	shame	She blushed with **shame** after she told the lie.	shame
8	dish	That fancy **dish** is very old.	dish
9	then	The cat drank the milk **then** licked its paws.	then
10	those	**Those** books belong to the library.	those
11	neck	He hurt his **neck** while playing football.	neck
12	this	**This** spelling test has twenty words.	this
13	chain	The **chain** on his bike is broken.	chain
14	both	Brittany broke **both** of her arms.	both
15	while	The mother cleaned the house **while** the baby slept.	while
16	chat	She likes to **chat** with her friend.	chat
17	their	The family loves **their** dog.	their
18	path	The bike **path** was very bumpy.	path
19	quiet	It is important to be **quiet** while taking a test.	quiet
20	whale	The **whale** is a very large animal.	whale

LANGUAGE ARTS 205

Unit 5: Using Punctuation

TEACHER NOTES

MATERIALS NEEDED FOR LIFEPAC	
Required	Suggested
• sharp pencil	• crayons or colored pencils • notebook or composition book for journaling • paper with guidelines for Spelling Tests

OPTIONAL ADDITIONAL LEARNING ACTIVITIES

This unit introduces biographies to the students. Use your favorite Bible Story book as an introduction to this unit. Ask the students who their favorite Bible character is. Ask them what they know about this character. Ask them how they know things about this character. Explain to them that when they read about a person's life, they are reading a biography.

Section 1

1. There are many people mentioned in the Bible. Some of these people have a lot written about them. You can read about Jesus in many books and chapters of the Bible. There are some books in the Bible that are written about one person. The book of Job has 42 chapters that tell about Job. You can learn about Job by reading all of those chapters. Sometimes we learn very little about a person in the Bible. Read Genesis 5:25–27. There are just three verses about a man named Methuselah, but we learn that Methuselah lived to be 969 years old! He lived the longest of any person that we know! There would be a lot of candles on his birthday cake!
2. Write these sentences (without punctuation marks) on the board or a large piece of paper:

   Can you read this
   These sentences do not have an ending punctuation mark
   What punctuation mark should be at the end
3. Read Acts 9:23–25 with the students. (Paul escaped with the help of his friends. They lowered him through a window down in a basket.) Talk about how large this basket was to hold Paul!

Section 2

1. Write the following words on cards. Have the students divide the cards/words into Word Families.

it	pit	sit	knit
ill	pill	sill	fill
in	pin	sin	fin
ate	date	gate	plate
at	bat	sat	fat
eat	beat	seat	neat
odd	clod	sod	cod
fun	sun	bun	nun

2. Review using commas in a list of a sentence. Write these sentences on a board or a large piece of paper:

   Jill put the paper doll, picture book, and crayons in the drawer. (3 things)
   Jill put the paper doll, picture, book, and crayons in the drawer. (4 things)
   Jill put the paper, doll, picture book, and crayons in the drawer. (4 things)
   Jill put the paper, doll, picture, book, and crayons in the drawer. (5 things)

   Show the students how the placement of commas in sentences changes the meaning.

Section 3

1. Discuss with the students the difference between singular and plural nouns.
2. Make the following chart on the board or a large piece of paper. Have the students place the following words under **singular** or **plural**: acorns, trees, leaf, peach, vine, bushes, berries, branch, poppy, daisies, grasses, lily

Singular	Plural

3. Guide the students in a discussion on a person that they wish to write a "mini-biography."
4. Discuss the following questions with the students:
   a. How old was Abraham when Isaac was born?
   b. What does the name Isaac mean?
   c. Who talked to Paul when he was walking to Damascus?
   d. Who made clothes for the poor people?
   e. Who made Tabitha alive again?
5. Remind the students that God created Isaac, Paul, the little boy that helped Jesus, and Tabitha. God also created you! You are very special to God. He loves you. Share the following interesting facts about the human body. (Students could also write these facts in their journals.)
   - Your eyes blink about 10 million times each year.
   - There are 54 bones in your hands and wrists.
   - You use 17 muscles to smile and 43 muscles to frown.
   - You have about 100,000 hairs on your head.
   - Fingernails grow faster than toenails.

Suggested Books:

Johnny Appleseed: A Tall Tale Retold and Illustrated by Steven Kellogg
Children's Book of Virtues by Bill Bennett
The Children's Book of Heroes by Bill Bennett

Journal Suggestions:

1. Refer to #5 of Section 3.
2. Have the students write in their journals about a favorite Bible character.

» WORKSHEET ANSWERS

Contractions Review:

Allison was at the house of her cousins. It was time to go to bed. Allison wished that it (wasn't) bedtime. She had a fun day with her cousins. She (didn't) want to go to bed. Aunt Cindy said that tomorrow they would play at the park. They (couldn't) go to the swimming pool. (It's) not going to be open. (They'll) have lots of fun at the park. They hope that it (doesn't) rain!

1. was not
2. did not
3. could not
4. it is
5. They will
6. does not

Series Comma Review:

1. c
2. 4
3. b
4. 3
5. a
6. 4

Administer the LIFEPAC Spelling Test.

Administer the LIFEPAC Test.

CONTRACTIONS REVIEW

Read the story.
Circle the words that are contractions. Write the two words for each contraction on the lines after the story.

Allison was at the house of her cousins. It was time to go to bed. Allison wished that it wasn't bedtime. She had a fun day with her cousins. She didn't want to go to bed. Aunt Cindy said that tomorrow they would play at the park. They couldn't go to the swimming pool. It's not going to be open. They'll have lots of fun at the park. They are hoping that it doesn't rain!

1. ____________________ 2. ____________________

3. ____________________ 4. ____________________

5. ____________________ 6. ____________________

SERIES COMMAS REVIEW

Put a check mark (✓) next to the sentence that has the commas in the correct places. Then answer the question.

1. ☐ a. Jon got a car truck baseball and bat for Christmas.

   ☐ b. Jon got a car, and truck, and baseball, and bat, for Christmas.

   ☐ c. Jon got a car, truck, baseball, and bat for Christmas.

2. How many things did Jon get for Christmas?____________

3. ☐ a. Mother gave Father a book, shirt, and, slippers, for Christmas.

   ☐ b. Mother gave Father a book, shirt, and slippers for Christmas.

   ☐ c. Mother gave Father a book, and shirt, and slippers for Christmas.

4. How many things did Mother give Father for Christmas?

   ____

5. ☐ a. Mother, Father, Jenny, and Jon had fun.

   ☐ b. Mother, and Father, and Jenny, and Jon, had fun.

   ☐ c. Mother Father Jenny and Jon had fun.

6. How many people had fun?____________

ANSWER KEYS

SECTION 1

1.1 Suggested answers:
- a. Abraham and Sarah
- b. 100 years old
- c. laughter
- d. an angel of God
- e. a ram
- f. Rebekah
- g. Jacob and Esau
- h. Genesis

1.2
1. Abraham and Sarah named their son Isaac.
2. Abraham and Isaac went up the mountain.
3. Isaac married Rebekah.

1.3 Possible answers:
- a. around
- b. count, crowd
- c. crowd, count
- d. crown
- e. found
- f. fowl, loud
- g. house
- h. loud, fowl
- i. noun
- j. owl
- k. town
- l. wow

1.4
t**oi**l
f**oi**l
oink
j**oi**n
n**oi**se

1.5
b**oy**
j**oy**
enj**oy**
ann**oy**
dec**oy**

1.6
- a. boy
- b. cowboy
- c. decoy
- d. oil
- e. choice
- f. enjoyed
- g. soil
- h. soybean
- i. spoil
- j. joy
- k. Loy
- l. coins

1.7
Roy
Roy is a boy. Roy had to make a choice. He had to choose which toy he would enjoy. Would he like a cowboy hat or a microphone that changed his voice? His mother foiled his plan. She gave him some gold coins, oil paints, and a duck decoy.

1.8 Teacher check

1.9
statement sentence ?
question sentence !
exclamation sentence .

(Lines on the page match statement sentence with ".", question sentence with "?", and exclamation sentence with "!".)

1.10
- a. .
- b. .
- c. .
- d. !, !
- e. ?
- f. .
- g. !, ! (*or* .)
- h. ?
- i. . (*or* !)

1.11 Teacher check

1.12
- a. owl
- b. wow
- c. loud
- d. noun
- e. fowl
- f. town
- g. count
- h. crowd
- i. crown
- j. found
- k. house
- l. around

1.13 Circled answers:
- a. Paul's real name was Saul.
- b. A bright light made Paul fall to the ground.
- c. The voice of Jesus talked to Paul.
- d. Paul could not see.
- e. Paul did not eat or drink for three days.
- f. Paul was baptized.
- g. Paul became a missionary.
- h. You can read about Paul in Acts 9.

1.14 Teacher check

1.15 The Proud Farmer

The proud farmer went to the barn to count his animals. He saw a cow, a sow, a mouse, a cat, and an owl all sitting on the ground by the plow.

Pow! Boom! There was a loud sound of thunder from a dark cloud. He was glad his animals were safe in the big old brown barn.

The farmer went back to his house, and his mouth began to water. He found his wife with her gown covered with flour. She was baking a pound cake in the oven

The farmer sat on the couch. He eagerly waited for the cake to come out of the oven. How excited he was to chow down on his wife's fine cooking!

Words with ow	**Words with ou**
cow	Proud
sow	proud
owl	count
plow	mouse
Pow	ground
brown	loud
gown	sound
How	cloud
chow	house
down	mouth
	found
	flour
	pound
	couch
	out

1.16 Any order:
- a. how, sow, plow, pow, chow
- b. loud, cloud
- c. gown, down
- d. found, pound, sound
- e. house

1.17 Teacher check

1.18
- a. Ernie and Fred went scuba diving.
- b. Where did they go scuba diving?
- c. The went scuba diving in Florida.
- d. What pretty fish they saw! (*or* .)
- e. Ernie saw several sea stars.
- f. Did Ernie show Fred the sea stars?
- g. They saw many brightly colored fish.
- h. What fun they had scuba diving! (*or* .)

SELF TEST 1

1.01 **oi**l
1.02 t**oy**
1.03 j**oi**n
1.04 b**oy**
1.05 dec**oy**
1.06 c**oi**n
1.07 s**oi**l
1.08 j**oy**
1.09 m**oi**st
1.010 – 1.013 Any order: toy, decoy, boy, joy
1.014 – 1.015 Either order: coin, join
1.016 ?
1.017 !
1.018 .
1.019 co**w**
1.020 lo**u**d
1.021 mo**u**se
1.022 o**w**l

SECTION 2

2.1 Possible answers:
a. boil
b. toy, boy
c. coin
d. employ
e. joint, point
f. joy
g. loyal
h. moist
i. oyster
j. point, joint
k. soil
l. boy, toy

2.2 Teacher check

2.3
[2] A little boy shared his lunch of five loaves and two fish.
[1] Jesus had talked to the people for a long time and they were hungry.
[4] There were twelve baskets of food left over.
[3] Jesus prayed to God and gave thanks for the food.

2.4
a. boil
b. boy
c. coin
d. employ
e. joint
f. joy
g. loyal
h. moist
i. oyster
j. point
k. soil
l. toy

2.5
a. coins
b. tooth
c. cloud
d. goat
e. pie
f. cow
g. hay
h. glue
i. feet
j. toy
k. pail
l. bean

2.6
a. hay b. bean
c. goat d. pie
e. tooth f. cow
g. feet h. pail
i. cloud j. toy
k. coins l. glue

2.7
a. boil b. boy
c. coin d. employ
e. joint f. joy
g. loyal h. moist
i. oyster j. point
k. soil l. toy

2.8 Teacher check

2.9 Rod, Lyle, Joe, and David went out for pizza.
a. four (4)
b. Rod, Lyle, Joe, and David

They had cheese, pepperoni, onions, and mushrooms on their pizza.
c. four (4)
d. cheese, pepperoni, onions, and mushrooms

2.10 a

2.11 a

2.12 b

2.13
a. Mother helped Jill, Kirk, Jake, and Jan plant a garden.
b. They planted beans, peas, radishes, lettuce, and beets in their garden.
c. They hoed, watered, weeded, fertilized, and marked the rows of seeds.
d. Mother picked roses, tulips, daisies, violets, and lilies to put in a vase.
e. Jill, Jan, and Mother put vases of flowers in several rooms of the house.
f. They put the flowers in the kitchen, family room, dining room, and bedroom.
g. Father, Kirk, and Jake got supper ready.
h. The family ate hamburgers, salad, carrots, celery, and watermelon for supper.
i. Father, Mother, Jill, Kirk, Jake, and Jan were tired when they went to bed.
j. The children brushed their teeth, put on their pajamas, and said their prayers before they went to bed.

2.14 Teacher check

2.15
[3] Tabitha's friends asked Peter to come.
[5] Tabitha was alive!
[1] Tabitha loved God and helped many people.
[4] Peter prayed and told Tabitha to get up.
[2] Tabitha became very sick and died.

2.16 Teacher check

SELF TEST 2

2.01

maid	tie
sweet	point
leaf	toy
lie	pouch
cool	today
boil	rain
road	clue
joy	steam
count	brown
how	green
clay	coat
true	fool

2.02 a
2.03 c
2.04 b
2.05 **oi**l
2.06 b**oi**l
2.07 j**oy**
2.08 b**oy**
2.09 c**oi**n
2.010 empl**oy**
2.011 m**oi**st
2.012 **oy**ster
2.013 p**oi**nt
2.014 s**oi**l

SECTION 3

3.1 a. blow
b. crow
c. dough
d. enough
e. should
f. slow
g. sow
h. thought
i. through
j. toward
k. would
l. your

3.2 *Red* (*ou*): grouch, pouch, round, couch, blouse, cloud, ground, noun, found, mouse, proud, sound
Blue (*long o͞o*): soup, you, group
Orange (*short ŭ*): tough, enough, touch
Purple (ô): thought, cough
Green (*long ō*): soul
Yellow (*short o͝o*): should, could, would

3.3 a. Show the dough to the fellow.
b. Know that the dough will grow.
c. The dough will grow though the bowl is cold.
d. Throw the dough below the bowl of the fellow.
e. Mow the grass below the snow.
f. Row the boat from below the willows.

3.4 a. cow b. crow
c. cow d. crow
e. crow f. cow

3.5 a. Could you go to the store?
b. I would like to go to the zoo.
c. Mom said I could go to the zoo if I would clean my room.
d. My group will go on a tour through the zoo.
e. I should do my best work in school.

3.6 a. I had to take a tough test at school today.
b. I thought very hard about some of the questions.
c. I studied enough and did not have a rough time with the test.
d. I ought to get a good grade on the test.

3.7 a. car**s** b. toy**s**
c. pen**s** d. leg**s**
e. boat**s** f. bean**s**
g. hawk**s** h. pet**s**

3.8 a. peach**es** b. ax**es**
c. dress**es** d. bush**es**
e. tax**es** f. beach**es**
g. wish**es** h. boss**es**

3.9 a. tray**s** b. play**s**
c. guy**s** d. buy**s**
e. stay**s** f. bay**s**
g. way**s** h. ray**s**

3.10 a. flies b. spies
c. pennies d. ponies
e. cities f. hobbies
g. stories h. puppies

3.11
child	geese
foot	children
goose	feet
ox	oxen
tooth	women
woman	teeth

3.12 a. bison
b. trout
c. swine
d. deer

3.13 a. foxes b. legs
c. guppies d. pets
e. deer f. beaches
g. men h. bushes
i. trays j. dresses

3.14 a. cars b. ladies
c. toys d. dishes
e. boats f. couches
g. pennies h. women
i. daisies j. deer
k. geese l. taxes
m. teeth n. hawks

3.15 blow
crow
dough
enough
should
slow
sow
thought
through
toward
would
your

3.16 Teacher check
3.17 Teacher check
3.18 Teacher check
3.19 Teacher check

3.20
you are	they've
let us	it's
it is	you're
should not	he'll
they have	shouldn't
he will	let's

would not	I'm
I am	can't
did not	she's
cannot	isn't
I will	wouldn't
we are	couldn't
she is	we're
you will	I'll
they are	aren't
could not	didn't
is not	you'll
I have	they're
are not	I've

3.21 Teacher check

3.22 a. is not o
b. he is i
c. I am a
d. could not o
e. we have h a
f. you are a
g. she will w i
h. does not o

3.23 a. **It's** a nice day for a field trip.
b. **We're** going to a pumpkin farm.
c. We **don't** have to travel far to get to the farm.
d. The teacher said we **can't** go in the corn maze.
e. Elsie **didn't** have any money for a pumpkin.
f. **She's** going to borrow money from me.
g. I **couldn't** decide which pumpkin I wanted.
h. There **isn't** room in the van for a large pumpkin.
i. **I'm** glad that we went to the pumpkin farm.

3.24 a. boyl boil
b. cownt count
c. dowgh dough
d. croun crown
e. joynt joint
f. joi joy
g. hows house
h. moyst moist
i. oister oyster
j. oul owl
k. wud would
l. toi toy

3.25 Teacher check

SELF TEST 3

3.01 sheep
3.02 dishes
3.03 men
3.04 papers
3.05 days
3.06 buses
3.07 moose
3.08 dogs
3.09 boxes
3.010 deer
3.011 forks
3.012 ponies
3.013 mice
3.014 inches
3.015 a. crow
b. cow
c. crow
d. crow
3.016 can't — cannot
won't — will not
it's — it is
we're — we are
3.017 b
3.018 a
3.019 b

UNIT REVIEW

1. Either order: would, could
2. Either order: through, soup
3. Either order: touch, enough
4. Either order: thought, ought
5. Either order: soul, though
6. A biography is a story about a person's life.
7. Jesus used a little boy's lunch to feed 5,000 people!
8. Paul's real name was Saul.
9. Did you know Tabitha was a kind woman?
10. ch**oi**ce
11. dec**oy**
12. j**oy**
13. **oi**nk
14. ann**oy**
15. c**oi**n
16. *green* (*ow as in cow*): chow, wow, gown, town, brown, owl
blue (*ow as in crow*): glow, snow, flow, blow, row, slow
17. a
18. 5
19. book — books
box — boxes
inch — inches
child — children
tray — trays
city — cities
foot — feet
sheep — sheep
puppy — puppies
tax — taxes
20. a. didn't
b. you'll
c. won't
d. I've

LIFEPAC TEST

1.

statement sentence	?
question sentence	!
exclamation sentence	.

2. biography
3.

Abraham was	twin sons named Esau and Jacob.
Isaac had	many books in the Bible.
Paul became	poor people.
Paul wrote	Isaac's father.
Tabitha helped	make Tabitha alive again.
God helped Peter	a great missionary for God.

4.

a. boy	boi	**boy**
b. joint	**joint**	joynt
c. enjoy	enjoi	**enjoy**
d. soil	**soil**	soyl

5. cl**ou**d
6. c**ow**
7. br**ow**n
8. m**ou**se
9. a
10. b
11. a
12. c
13. Any order: soup, four, your, show
14. cars
15. dishes
16. toys
17. ladies
18. teeth
19. deer
20. It's
21. They're
22. didn't
23. doesn't
24. won't

ALTERNATE LIFEPAC TEST

1. ?
2. .
3. ! !
4. biography
5. Abraham
6. Jacob
7. Paul
8. blind
9. poor people
10. Peter
11. p**oi**nt
12. t**oy**
13. b**oi**l
14. **oy**ster
15. a. loud
    b. town
    c. round
    d. gown
16. b
17. a
18. c
19. c
20. Any order:
    a. group b. slow
    c. you d. pour
21. a. legs
    b. beaches
    c. trays
    d. pennies
    e. feet
    f. moose
22. isn't
23. doesn't
24. can't
25. they'll

SPELLING TEST

1	dough	Greg helped his mother make bread **dough**.	dough
2	loyal	A dog can be a **loyal** pet.	loyal
3	crowd	There was a large **crowd** at the football game.	crowd
4	crow	A **crow** was eating the farmer's corn.	crow
5	owl	The **owl** flew around the barn at night.	owl
6	boil	Grandmother will **boil** water for tea.	boil
7	blow	The wind will **blow** through the open window.	blow
8	coin	The pirate found a gold **coin** on the ship.	coin
9	fowl	A pheasant is a wild **fowl**.	fowl
10	sow	The farmer will **sow** the seeds in the spring.	sow
11	moist	The cake that grandmother made was good and **moist**.	moist
12	noun	A **noun** is a word that is a person, place, or thing.	noun
13	thought	Amanda **thought** she could go to her friend's house.	thought
14	boy	The **boy** liked to play catch with his dad.	boy
15	found	The girl **found** her cat in the garage.	found
16	slow	The **slow** turtle walked along the beach.	slow
17	oyster	An **oyster** can make a pearl.	oyster
18	house	They painted their **house** a bright green.	house
19	toward	They raced **toward** the finish line.	toward
20	soil	The rich **soil** grew wonderful crops.	soil

LANGUAGE ARTS 205

ALTERNATE LIFEPAC TEST

Name ______________________

Date ______________________

Each answer = 1 point

Read the sentences.
Put the correct punctuation at the end of each sentence.

. ? !

1. What time is it ____
2. It is time for lunch ____
3. Yay____ I love pizza for lunch ____

Write the word that correctly completes each sentence.

4. A ______________________ is a story about a person's life.
(biome / biography)

5. ______________________ was Isaac's father.
(Abraham / Paul)

6. Isaac had twin sons named Esau and ________________ .
(Paul / Jacob)

7. ________________________ became a great missionary.
(Abraham / Paul)

8. Paul became __________________ .
(blind / deaf)

9. Tabitha helped ___________________________ .
(rich people / poor people)

10. God helped ________________________ make Tabitha alive again.
(Peter / Abraham)

Write the letters *oi* or *oy* on the lines to correctly spell the words.

11. p ____ ____nt

12. t ____ ____

13. b ____ ____l

14. ____ ____ster

Choose the correct way to spell the *ou* or *ow* words.
Write the correct spelling on the line.

15.
a. loud lowd ____________________
b. toun town ____________________
c. round rownd ____________________
d. goun gown ____________________

Circle the letter of each sentence that has the commas in the correct places.

16. a. The, zoo, has, giraffes, elephants, and, monkeys.
b. The zoo has giraffes, elephants, and monkeys.
c. The zoo has giraffes, and elephants, and, monkeys.

17. a. The zookeeper feeds the animals in the morning, afternoon, and evening.
b. The zookeeper feeds the animals in the morning, and afternoon, and, evening.
c. The zookeeper feeds the animals in the morning afternoon and evening.

18. a. The animals eat grass fruits, and vegetables.
b. The animals, eat, grass, fruits, and vegetables.
c. The animals eat grass, fruits, and vegetables.

19. a. Grandparents, and parents, and children, like to go to the zoo.
b. Grandparents, parents, and children, like to go to the zoo.
c. Grandparents, parents, and children like to go to the zoo.

Read the words below.
Write the words that do not make the *ow* sound as in *cow*.

group	pour	fowl	slow	you	proud	loud	couch

20. a. ______________ b. ______________

c. ______________ d. ______________

Choose the correct way to write the plural noun and write it on the line.

21.

a.	leg	______________	leges	legs
b.	beach	______________	beaches	beachs
c.	tray	______________	traies	trays
d.	penny	______________	pennies	pennys
e.	foot	______________	feet	foots
f.	moose	______________	mooses	moose

Read the sentences.
Write a contraction for the underlined words.

22. Jenna is not feeling well. ______________

23. She does not want to go to the doctor. ______________

24. Mother cannot take her this morning. ______________

25. They will go in the afternoon. ______________

ALTERNATE SPELLING TEST

1	around	The runners ran **around** the track.	around
2	enough	There was not **enough** flour to make cookies.	enough
3	employ	He will **employ** three people to mow his lawn.	employ
4	count	He can **count** to one hundred.	count
5	through	He ran **through** the house with dirty shoes.	through
6	toy	Jay got a **toy** fire truck for his birthday.	toy
7	loud	The **loud** music made the baby cry.	loud
8	should	You **should** not run with scissors.	should
9	joint	Your elbow is a hinge **joint**.	joint
10	crown	The queen's **crown** had many diamonds.	crown
11	your	It is important to brush **your** teeth.	your
12	joy	A cheerful smile can bring **joy** to a person.	joy
13	town	A **town** is smaller than a city.	town
14	would	She **would** love to have a birthday party.	would
15	point	It is impolite to **point** at someone.	point
16	wow	She said, "**Wow**! That is a beautiful bracelet."	wow
17	dough	Bradley likes to eat cookie **dough**.	dough
18	coin	Suzy got a silver **coin** for her graduation.	coin
19	crowd	The **crowd** cheered for the football team.	crowd
20	owl	An **owl** likes to hunt at night.	owl

LANGUAGE ARTS 206

Unit 6: Adjectives

TEACHER NOTES

MATERIALS NEEDED FOR LIFEPAC	
Required	Suggested
• sharp pencil	• crayons or colored pencils • notebook or composition book for journaling • paper with guidelines for Spelling Tests

OPTIONAL ADDITIONAL LEARNING ACTIVITIES

This is a unit about poetry. Begin this unit by reading your favorite poem to the students (or choose a poem from the selection list). Have several books of poetry available for the students to read or you can read some of the books to them.

Section 1

1. Share with the students some Bible songs (such as "The B-i-b-l-e" or some of your personal favorites.) Guide the students in discovering the rhyming words of the song.
2. Find some finger plays or jump rope rhymes to share with the children.
3. Art Activity: Have students illustrate their favorite Nursery Rhyme (or students could write the Nursery Rhyme in the journal with their illustration).
4. Say these words to the students: beach, peach, reach, teach, preach, bleach. Tell the students to think about these words. How are these words alike? They all have the word *each* in them. They are rhyming words. Have a student say a word to you—you tell them a rhyming word for the word that they said. Then you say a word to the students. Have them tell you a rhyming word that goes with the words you said.
5. Write the following nouns and verbs on the board or a large piece of paper. Have the students match the noun and a verb to make a very simple sentence to demonstrate subject and verb agreement:

Cows	moo
Stars	twinkle
Eyes	blink
Girls	smile
Dogs	bark
Motorcycles	zoom
Butterflies	fly
Snakes	slither

Section 2

1. Read Psalm 136:1–9 (from student's workbook) as an antiphonal psalm. Teacher reads the first line of each verse, and students read the next line: "His love endures forever."
2. Make simple musical instruments out of ordinary household items. Read Psalm 150 (from student's workbook) together with the students, playing the instruments with verses 3-5.
3. Have the students add a rhyming word to the following sentences to make couplets:

   I like to sing and play
   Each and every ____________________ .

   The little baby's name is Tom.
   When he cries, he wants his _______________ .

   Supper is cooking in a pot.
   Don't touch it though, because it is ______________ .

   If you get scared during the night,
   Have no fear; turn on the _______________________ .

   The wind is just right
   To fly my new ________________ .

Section 3

1. Read Ecclesiastes 3:1–11 to the students. Tell them to listen to a word that is repeated in this passage of Scripture (it is the word *time*). Explain to the students that poems sometimes have words that are repeated.
2. Poem recitation or memorization: Tell the students to find a poem that they really enjoy. Have the students practice reading this poem several times. You may have the students memorize the poem or nearly have it memorized. Tell them to use facial expressions or hand gestures with the poem. Tell them to practice the poem in front of a mirror. Have the students present the poems to the class.

   (Interpretive reading) A good poem for students to read is "Sick" by Shel Silverstein. (A demonstration by the teacher reading or reciting a poem would be good for example purposes.)
3. Choose a simple, fun poem for the students to memorize (can refer to the list of poems).
4. The shortest poem is: I

   Why?

   Write this shortest poem on the board or a large piece of paper and have the students read the poem. Tell the students that we as Christians can answer the question of why we are here on this earth. We are here because God created us, and we are to live to glorify and praise Him. (Keep this explanation simple for second graders.)

Suggested Books:

(This is list of suggested poems from *Core Knowledge Sequence: Content Guidelines for Grades K-8*)

Bad in Summer by Robert Louis Stevenson
Caterpillars by Aileen Fisher
Discovery by Harry Behn
Harriet Tubman by Eloise Greenfield
Hurt No Living Thing by Christina Rossetti
Lincoln by Nancy Byrd Turner
Rudolph is Tired of the City by Gwendolyn Brooks
Smart by Shel Silverstein
Something Told the Wild Geese by Rachel Field
There Was an Old Man with a Beard by Edward Lear
Who Has Seen the Wind by Christina Georgina Rossetti (in student's Unit 6)
Windy Nights by Robert Louis Stevenson

Journal Suggestions:

1. Let the students choose a favorite nursery rhyme. Have the students write and illustrate the rhyme in their journal.
2. Write some rhyming couplets as a class. Tell students to write the couplets in their journals.

» WORKSHEET ANSWERS

Contractions Review:

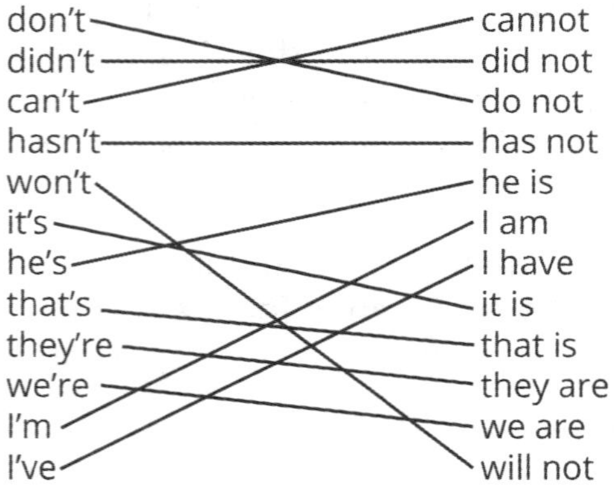

Administer the LIFEPAC Spelling Test.
The test is provided in this Teacher's Guide.
Evaluate the tests and review the words the students spelled incorrectly.
If necessary, review all of the words in the unit to prepare for the alternate spelling test.
Administer the Alternate LIFEPAC Spelling test that is provided in this Teacher's Guide.

Administer the LIFEPAC Test.
The test is to be administered in one session. Give no help except with directions.
Evaluate the tests and review areas where the students have done poorly.
Review the pages and activities that stress the concepts tested.
If necessary, administer the Alternate LIFEPAC Test.

CONTRACTIONS REVIEW

Draw a line to match the contractions with the words.

don't ▶	◀ cannot
didn't ▶	◀ did not
can't ▶	◀ do not
hasn't ▶	◀ has not
won't ▶	◀ he is
it's ▶	◀ I am
he's ▶	◀ I have
that's ▶	◀ it is
they're ▶	◀ that is
we're ▶	◀ they are
I'm ▶	◀ we are
I've ▶	◀ will not

ANSWER KEYS

SECTION 1

1.1 Possible answers:
- a. can't, won't
- b. I've
- c. didn't
- d. we're
- e. don't
- f. hasn't
- g. I'm
- h. it's
- i. he's
- j. won't, can't
- k. that's
- l. they're

1.2 Any order:
lice, rice, twice, slice, dice, price, mice, nice

1.3 Any order:
race, lace

1.4 Any order:
ran, man

1.5 Any order:
rest, nest

1.6 Any order:
mine, nine, line, twine, dine

1.7 Any order:
rope, mope, nope

1.8 Any order:
pray, ray, may, nay, lay, slay

1.9 Any order:
mad, lad

1.10 brush, flush, gush, hush, lush, mush, rush, thrush

1.11 bent, cent, dent, rent, sent, spent, tent, went

1.12 chop, cop, drop, mop, pop, shop, stop, top

1.13 chin, fin, grin, pin, sin, spin, thin, win

1.14

I'm I am	i'ts it is	isno't is not	w'll we will	youll you will	can't cannot
aren't are not	Iw'ill I will	we'll we will	I've I have	areno't are not	don't do not
she's she is	willn't will not	shew'ill she will	wasn't was not	weh've we have	they're they are
he'll he will	haven'ot have not	they'll they will	youh've you have	we'are we are	hasn't has not

1.15 Any order:

it's	we'll
I'll	you've
won't	you'll
haven't	aren't
isn't	we've
she'll	we're

1.16
- a. Jill **can't** go to school today.
- b. She **isn't** feeling well.
- c. The other children **don't** want to get sick.
- d. Jill's brother **hasn't** gotten her homework.
- e. He said **he's** going to mow the lawn.
- f. **I'm** going to watch him.
- g. **I've** a new lawn mower.
- h. **It's** in the garage.
- i. **That's** where we like to keep it.
- j. I think that **they're** going to like their new mower.
- k. **We're** happy with our new mower.
- l. The old mower **won't** start.

1.17 #1 Twinkle, twinkle, little star,
How I wonder what you are.
#2 Up above the world so high,
Like a diamond in the sky.
#3 Twinkle, twinkle, little star,
How I wonder what you are.
Teacher check

1.18 Teacher check

1.19 See below:

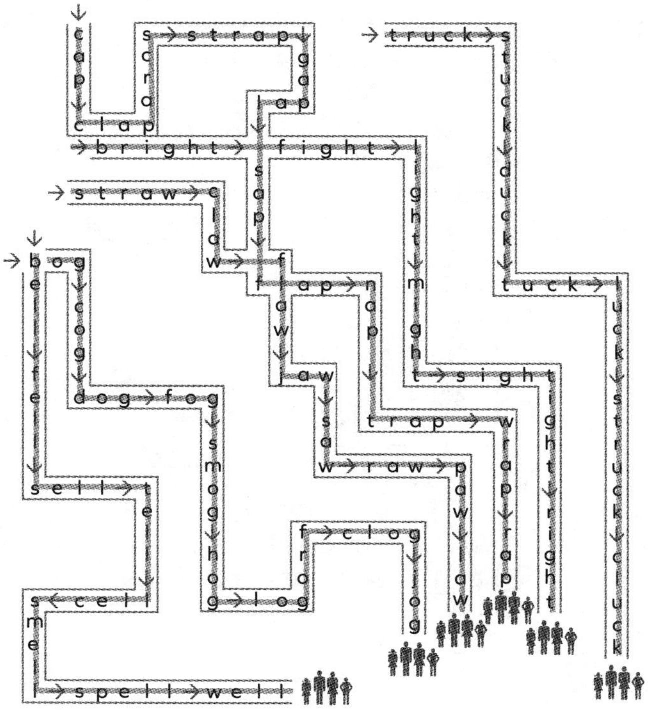

1.20 Any order within categories:

a. cap, clap, scrap, strap, gap, lap, sap, flap, nap, trap, wrap, rap

b. bog, cog, dog, fog, smog, hog, log, frog, clog, jog

c. straw, claw, flaw, jaw, saw, raw, paw, law

d. bell, fell, sell, tell, cell, smell, spell, well

e. truck, stuck, duck, tuck, luck, struck, cluck

f. bright, fight, light, might, sight, tight, right

1.21 Teacher check

1.22
a. boy
b. saw
c. girl
d. caught
e. man
f. drove
g. horse
h. ran

1.23
a. The fish swam in the water.
b. The boy played a game.
c. The bride wore a dress.
d. The monkey wore a hat.
e. The cow ate the corn.
f. The baby drank the juice.

1.24
a. The colorful fish swam in the water.
The colorful fish swam in the clear water.
b. The young boy played a game.
The young boy played a video game.
c. The happy bride wore a dress.
The happy bride wore a wedding dress.
d. The silly monkey wore a hat.
The silly monkey wore a yellow hat.
e. The big cow ate corn.
The big cow ate sweet corn.
f. The cute baby drank juice.
The cute baby drank apple juice.

SELF TEST 1

Any order:

1.01 Word Family **ame**:
came, same, name

Word Family **eel**:
peel, feel, wheel

Word Family **am**:
slam, ham, jam

Word Family **in**:
pin, shin, win

Word Family **eet**:
sleet, feet, sweet

Word Family **ine**:
pine, vine, shine

1.02 S
1.03 V
1.04 V
1.05 S
1.06 A
1.07 A
1.08 N
1.09 N
1.010 A
1.011 Ben — loves to fish.
Ben's dad — took Ben fishing.

SECTION 2

2.1 Possible answers:
a. sank
b. plank
c. hall
d. call, cold
e. ship, whip
f. whip, ship
g. right, night
h. cold, call
i. night, right
j. gold
k. den
l. been

2.2 Teacher check

2.3 Teacher check

2.4 See below:

z	y	d	x	w	n	v	u	q
b	e	e	n	r	i	g	h	t
f	g	n	j	k	g	c	p	r
c	o	l	d	z	h	a	l	l
z	l	k	w	q	t	l	s	y
b	d	s	h	i	p	l	a	l
r	q	u	i	v	w	x	n	z
o	n	m	p	l	a	n	k	u

2.5 Suggested answers:
a. **b**all b. **c**all c. **d**all
d. **f**all e. **g**all f. **h**all
g. **j**ail h. **k**all i. **l**all
j. **m**all k. **n**all l. **p**all
m. **q**all n. **r**all o. **s**all
p. **t**all q. **v**all r. **w**all
s. **x**all t. **y**all u. **z**all

2.6 Suggested answers:
a. **b**at b. **c**at c. **d**at
d. **f**at e. **g**at f. **h**at
g. **j**at h. **k**at i. **l**at
j. **m**at k. **n**at l. **p**at
m. **q**at n. **r**at o. **s**at
p. **t**at q. **v**at r. **w**at
s. **x**at t. **y**at u. **z**at

2.7 a. **o**at b. **e**at

2.8 a. **b**ow b. **c**ow c. **d**ow
d. **f**ow e. **g**ow f. **h**ow
g. **j**ow h. **k**ow i. **l**ow
j. **m**ow k. **n**ow l. **p**ow
m. **q**ow n. **r**ow o. **s**ow
p. **t**ow q. **v**ow r. **w**ow
s. **x**ow t. **y**ow u. **z**ow

2.9 a. **fl**all, **fl**at, **fl**ow
b. **ch**all, **ch**at, **ch**ow
c. **th**all, **th**at, **th**ow
d. **wh**all, **wh**at, **wh**ow

2.10 flat, chat, that
flow, chow, what

2.11 a. no
b. yes
c. no

2.12

fill	sheep
Anna	Will
ate	sing
Sandy	Hannah
keep	Andy
ring	cat
hat	date
pig	wig

2.13 a. den
b. right
c. ship
d. sank
e. gold
f. hall

2.14 a. maple
b. old
c. joyful
d. yellow
e. cherry
f. tennis
g. silly
h. seven
i. little
j. six

2.15 adjectives

2.16 a. little
b. hidden
c. his
d. four
e. treasure
f. long
g. golden
h. their
i. fun

2.17 Teacher check
2.18 Teacher check
2.19 for his mercy endureth forever
2.20 Psalm 150

(Praise) ye the LORD. (Praise) God in his sanctuary: (praise) him in the firmament of his power.

(Praise) him for his mighty acts: (praise) him according to his excellent greatness.

(Praise) him with the sound of the trumpet: (praise) him with psaltery and harp.

(Praise) him with the timbrel and dance: (praise) him with stringed instruments and organs.

(Praise) him upon the loud cymbals; (praise) him upon the high sounding cymbals.

Let everything that hath breath (praise) the LORD. (Praise) ye the LORD.

praise

2.21 Teacher check
2.22 Teacher check
2.23
a. in side
b. after noon
c. back yard
d. news paper
e. fire place
f. pony tail
g. suit case
h. play ground

2.24
a. airport
b. crosswalk
c. dragonfly
d. earthquake
e. headlight
f. jellyfish
g. playpen
h. popcorn
i. sailboat
j. scarecrow
k. teacup
l. toothbrush
m. upstairs
n. whirlpool

SELF TEST 2

2.01 Couplet 1 rhyming words: bright, tonight
Couplet 2 rhyming words: might, tonight

2.02 Couplet 1 rhyming words: horn, corn
Couplet 2 rhyming words: sheep, asleep
Couplet 3 rhyming words: I, cry

2.03 Suggested answers – any three: pat, fat, hat, cat, sat, rat, mat
2.04 Suggested answers – any three: coat, oat, goat, tote, note, moat, vote
2.05 sunny
2.06 pretty
2.07 big
2.08 Her
2.09 colorful
2.010 backyard
2.011 sunflowers
2.012 sandbox
2.013 bumblebees
2.014 butterfly

SECTION 3

3.1
a. upon
b. outside
c. sometimes
d. mailbox
e. raincoat
f. pigpen
g. baseball
h. birthday
i. without
j. notebook
k. beehive
l. waterfall

3.2
a. Jane is **faster** than Mary.
b. A turtle is **slower** than a rabbit.
c. Mike is **taller** than Joe.
d. Joe is **shorter** than Mike.
e. I am **older** than my brother.

3.3
a. Mary, Kay, and Ann are tall, but Jane is the **tallest**.
b. A turtle and a snail are slow, but the sloth is the **slowest** animal of all.

3.4
a. large
b. larger
c. largest
d. sweet
e. sweeter
f. sweetest
g. tall
h. taller
i. tallest
j. bright
k. brighter
l. brightest

3.5 Teacher check

3.6 See below:

bad	bat	day	date	**dad**	tap	tape	bear
coat	cool	too	**boat**	cot	**goat**	crow	clap
cool	cold	**pool**	clock	cod	coat	**tool**	new
jog	**hog**	joke	go	huge	jump	joy	**dog**
eel	**peel**	meet	**feel**	seat	**wheel**	let	**heel**
rain	**train**	ran	pin	king	rink	fit	**pain**
pack	**back**	cake	came	duck	pad	pay	**sack**
claw	**paw**	few	clue	pause	now	clack	**raw**
tide	**wide**	tie	die	team	dad	rude	**ride**
cow	**how**	come	**now**	few	**wow**	cave	**vow**
wing	**sing**	song	wide	**thing**	hang	fang	**king**
mile	miss	**smile**	mole	mill	rail	**pile**	rule
tame	take	tale	**game**	time	**name**	tire	type
bat	batter	bait	ate	**cat**	date	past	bag

3.7 a smiley face

3.8
a. shoe
b. star
c. fox
d. mouse
e. head
f. bark
g. clock

3.9

base	ball
bee	book
birth	box
mail	coat
note	day
out	fall
pig	hive
rain	pen
some	on
up	out
water	side
with	times

3.10
a. noun
b. verb
c. singular
d. plural
e. adjective
f. statement
g. question
h. exclamation

3.11
a. middle
b. large
c. rush
d. wealthy
e. damp
f. lady
g. little
h. huge

3.12
a. outside
b. little
c. slow
d. poor
e. dry
f. man
g. big
h. tiny

3.13
a. synonym
b. antonym
c. antonym
d. synonym
e. synonym
f. antonym
g. antonym
h. synonym
i. synonym
j. synonym

3.14
a. fond
b. acorn, cavity, eaglet
c. bake, describe
d. eaglet
e. eaglet, cavity

3.15
a. eaglet
b. acorn
c. bake
d. fond
e. cavity
f. describe

3.16 Teacher check

3.17 Austin went to the pet store. He wanted a little gerbil. He saw six gerbils. He chose a brown gerbil.
Suggested answers:
a. the pet store
b. little
c. six
d. brown

3.18 Possible answers – Teacher check:
good/lovely
lovely
pleasant/friendly
friendly/kind
pleasant/friendly/wonderful

3.19 Teacher check

3.20

a.	cann't	can't
b.	outsied	outside
c.	rite	right
d.	malebox	mailbox
e.	willn't	won't
f.	golde	gold
g.	he'is	he's
h.	burthday	birthday
i.	withowt	without
j.	wer'e	we're
k.	planck	plank
l.	watterfal	waterfall

SELF TEST 3

3.01 older
3.02 tallest
3.03 moist
3.04 quicker
3.05 newer
3.06 go
3.07 king
3.08 shoe
3.09 head
3.010 Suggested answer – toy
3.011 noun
3.012 comparative
3.013 verb
3.014 superlative
3.015 rain – fall
bee – hive
jelly – fish
note – book
3.016 S
3.017 A
3.018 S
3.019 A
3.020 many
3.021 long
3.022 My

UNIT REVIEW

1. Teacher check
2. don't
3. can't
4. she's
5. we're
6. verb
7. adjective
8. noun
9. (Any appropriate rhyming answer)
10. (Any appropriate rhyming answer)
11. (Any appropriate answer)
12. (Any appropriate answer)
13. (Any appropriate answer)

14.	sunflower	sun	flower
15.	butterfly	butter	fly
16.	dragonfly	dragon	fly
17.	sunshine	sun	shine

18. Lee is a faster runner than Jan.
19. The whale is the large of all sea animals.
20. A big tree fell on the car.
21. Holly is the shortest girl of the three girls in her family.
22-29. Suggested answers:
22. glad
23. fast
24. giggle
25. kind
26. cold
27. girl
28. light
29. sad

LIFEPAC TEST

1. couplet
2. adjective
3. compound word
4. contractions
5. bed
6. head
7. lay
8. hay
9. test
10. day
11. bean
12. one
13. brown
14. six
15. Her
16. sad
17. pin
18. cap
19. hot
20. top
21. birth — ball
    basket — side
    in — book
    note — day
22. blue
23. six
24. slower
25. slow
26. grin
27. fast
28. silly
29. big
30. frown
31. slow
32. sad
33. little

ALTERNATE LIFEPAC TEST

1. b
2. a
3. d
4. c
5. rise
6. wise
7. rise
8. wise
9. toy
10. hair
11. seen
12. gold
13. Her
14. red
15. four
16. face
17. fit
18. sheep
19. hut
20. told
21. bird — ball
    foot — side
    out — bath
    play — ground
22. five
23. red
24. fast
25. faster
26. wealthy
27. close
28. speedy
29. big
30. poor
31. far
32. slow
33. small

SPELLING TEST

1	we're	**We're** going to the beach tomorrow.	we're
2	night	I like to watch the stars at **night**.	night
3	mailbox	There were many letters in the **mailbox**.	mailbox
4	won't	Fido **won't** go in his doghouse.	won't
5	gold	**Gold** is a valuable metal.	gold
6	can't	He **can't** go to the zoo.	can't
7	sometimes	**Sometimes** Angela likes to eat cold pizza.	sometimes
8	ship	The sailors liked sailing the large **ship**.	ship
9	beehive	The bees were buzzing around the **beehive**.	beehive
10	didn't	I **didn't** do it!	didn't
11	den	Daniel was in the lion's **den**.	den
12	pigpen	He cleaned the **pigpen**.	pigpen
13	that's	**That's** one spicy meatball.	that's
14	cold	It is **cold** in South Dakota in the winter.	cold
15	birthday	She was excited for her **birthday** party.	birthday
16	he's	**He's** going to her party.	he's
17	right	He knew the **right** answer to the question.	right
18	waterfall	They got wet when they were by the **waterfall**.	waterfall
19	hasn't	He **hasn't** a clue how to fix the car.	hasn't
20	sank	The ship **sank** in the ocean.	sank

LANGUAGE ARTS 206

ALTERNATE LIFEPAC TEST

Name ______________________

Date ______________________

Each answer = 1 point

Read the words.
Write the letter of the correct answer on the line by the definition.

a. adjective b. couplet
c. compound d. contractions

1. ________ two lines of poetry with rhyming words at the end of the lines

2. ________ a word that describes a noun

3. ________ can't, I've, she's

4. ________ a word that is two words made into one word

Read the Mother Goose rhyme below.
Write the rhyming words of the couplets on the lines.

Cocks crow in the morn to tell us to rise,
And he who lies late will never be wise.
For early to bed and early to rise
Is the way to be healthy and wise.

5. ______________________ **6.** ______________________

7. ______________________ **8.** ______________________

Use the words below to complete the couplets.

gold	hair	seen	toy

9. Look at the boy
Play with his ______________________ .

10. That little girl over there
Has a ribbon in her ______________________ .

11. The grass is turning green,
Signs of spring can be ______________________ .

12. The weather was cold
When the pirates found the ______________________ .

Read the sentences. Circle the adjective that describes the underlined noun in each sentence.

13. Her dog ran away.

14. Billy wore a red shirt.

15. Sara ate four carrots.

Circle the word that rhymes with the underlined word.

16.	race	face	rate
17.	sit	site	fit
18.	deep	sheep	deer
19.	cut	cute	hut
20.	bold	told	bald

Draw a line between the two words that make a compound word.

21.	bird ▸	◂ ball
	foot ▸	◂ side
	out ▸	◂ bath
	play ▸	◂ ground

Write the correct adjective on the line.

22. That cat has ________________ kittens.
(red / five)

23. Ted saw a _____________ fire truck.
(red / five)

24. The lion is a ____________________ animal.
(fast / faster)

25. The shark swims ___________________ than a sea turtle.
(fast / faster)

Circle the correct *synonym* for the underlined word.

26.	<u>rich</u>	poor	wealthy
27.	<u>near</u>	close	far
28.	<u>fast</u>	speedy	slow
29.	<u>large</u>	small	big

Circle the correct *antonym* for the underlined word.

30.	<u>rich</u>	poor	wealthy
31.	<u>near</u>	close	far
32.	<u>fast</u>	speedy	slow
33.	<u>large</u>	small	big

ALTERNATE SPELLING TEST

1	baseball	He plays first base on his **baseball** team.	baseball
2	call	She tried to **call** her grandmother.	call
3	don't	**Don't** you want some chocolate chip cookies?	don't
4	raincoat	It looked like it was going to rain so she took her **raincoat**.	raincoat
5	hall	He ran down the **hall** to his bedroom.	hall
6	I'm	**I'm** going to read my library book.	I'm
7	without	He rode his bike **without** training wheels.	without
8	plank	Their diving board was made of a long, wooden **plank**.	plank
9	it's	**It's** fun to go swimming on a hot day.	it's
10	outside	The cat slept **outside** last night.	outside
11	they're	**They're** going out for supper tonight.	they're
12	upon	You can depend **upon** Jim to get the job done.	upon
13	been	He hasn't **been** to the dentist for a long time.	been
14	I've	**I've** never been to Alaska.	I've
15	sometimes	**Sometimes** we play games after supper.	sometimes
16	whip	The cruel warrior used a **whip** on the horse.	whip
17	beehive	There was honey in the **beehive**.	beehive
18	right	It's always **right** to tell the truth.	right
19	he's	**He's** on the softball team.	he's
20	notebook	She liked to draw pictures in her **notebook**.	notebook

LANGUAGE ARTS 207

Unit 7: Possessive Nouns

TEACHER NOTES

MATERIALS NEEDED FOR LIFEPAC	
Required	Suggested
• sharp pencil	• crayons or colored pencils • notebook or composition book for journaling • dictionary • blank address labels • paper with guidelines for Spelling Tests

OPTIONAL ADDITIONAL LEARNING ACTIVITIES

This is a unit on letter writing. You could begin this unit by reading the book by Alma Flor Ada: *Dear Peter Rabbit*. This book has examples of letters that the students could look at.

Section 1

1. Make a poster of a sample letter with the five parts of the letter labeled. (You may use a letter from the student's workbook.)
2. Make a poster of a sample envelope.
3. Have the students memorize their addresses (if they haven't done so already). Have them practice writing their addresses correctly.
4. Have the students make mailboxes out of shoeboxes. Have plenty of envelopes and paper available for students to write each other letters. A student can be assigned to be a mail carrier for the day and deliver the letters to the mailboxes. (Use address labels for students to create or design their own postage stamp to use on the letters that they send in the class.)

Section 2

1. Hand out dictionaries to each student. Have the students just look through the dictionary. Ask them where they would find the word *ape* in the dictionary. Discuss with them that they would find the word *ape* at the beginning of the dictionary because the word *ape* begins with the letter *a*. Have them find the word *ape*. Have the students find the last entry word in the dictionary. Ask them what letter this word begins with.
2. Have a friendly contest with the students. Say a word and have the students find the word in the dictionary. The student that can tell you the page that the word is found earns one point. The student with the most points wins!
3. Discuss with the students that 1 Corinthians 13 from the Bible is called the "Love Chapter," written by Paul to the Christians in a place called Corinth. Read 1 Corinthians 13 with the students. Explain to the students that people in Bible times wrote their letters on special paper and rolled it up in a scroll to be delivered. Have the students write 1 Corinthians 13:12–13 on a piece of paper. Roll the piece of paper to look like a scroll. The students can pretend that this is a letter to them.

1 Corinthians 13:12-13

For now we see through a glass, darkly;
but then face to face: now I know in part;
but then shall I know even as also I am known.
And now abideth faith, hope, charity, these three;
but the greatest of these is charity.

Section 3

1. Hand out the dictionaries to each student. Allow the students to explore the dictionary, find new words, look at illustrations, find specified words, etc.
2. Direct the students to look at the pronunciation key in the dictionary. Review with the students the purpose of and how to use the pronunciation key.
3. Paul wrote many letters to his friends. Paul's friends probably wrote letters back to Paul. When friends write letters to each other they are called pen pals. Do you have a pen pal? You can be a pen pal to a friend who has moved. You can be a pen pal to a cousin. Sometimes a pen pal can be from a different country. Sometimes a pen pal can be someone that you never met. Talk to your parents or an adult friend if you would like to have a pen pal. They can help you find one. You could even write a letter to a child in a missionary family. Pray for your pen pal just as Paul prayed for his pen pals. Remember that God loves and cares for your pen pal. Thank God for your pen pal!

   The best way to teach this unit is to write letters. The student will be assigned to write a letter in this unit's lessons. Please encourage the student to write another letter.

Suggested Books:

The Jolly Postman by Janet and Allan Ahlberg
The Jolly Christmas Postman by Janet and Allan Ahlberg
Toot and Puddle by Holly Hobbie
Letters from Felix: A Little Rabbit on a World Tour by Annette Langen
Dear Peter Rabbit: A Story with Real Miniature Letters by Beatrix Potter
The Gardener by Sarah Stewart
Dear Mrs. LaRue: Letters from Obedience School by Mark Teague

Journal Suggestions:

1. Tell the students to write a letter in their journals to the Bible character that they wrote about from the previous unit.

Administer the LIFEPAC Spelling Test.

Administer the LIFEPAC Test.

ANSWER KEYS

SECTION 1

1.1

2424 Sunrise Street
Chandler, MN 12368

August 21, 20 ___
Dear Pete,

I am doing fine. I spend lots of time in the garden. The corn likes the hot, hot weather, but so do the weeds! *or* . Soon it will be time to pick all the vegetables. Would you like to come over and help?

I am glad that your tooth did not hurt when it fell out. Does it feel funny to have a new space in your mouth? It must be hard to eat apples now. You will have to try applesauce instead! *or* .

Love,
Grandma

1.2 Possible answers:
a. age
b. cage
c. cause, raise
d. cent
e. city
f. does, lace
g. gem
h. gym
i. lace, does
j. please
k. raise, cause
l. slice

1.3

gem	kāj
cage	jə-**răf**
gerbil	jĕm
giant	jĭm
giraffe	**jûr**-bəl
gym	**jī**-ənt

1.4

cent	lās
rice	fĕns
fence	**pĕn**-səl
pencil	sĕnt
juice	rīs
lace	jo͞os

1.5
a. is b. was
c. hers d. those
e. does f. as
g. his h. words

1.6
a. gra**ph** b. go**ph**er
c. or**ph**an d. dol**ph**in
e. al**ph**abet f. **ph**one

1.7
a. cou**gh** b. tou**gh**
c. lau**gh** d. rou**gh**
e. enou**gh** f. trou**gh**

1.8 Teacher check

1.9

noun	shows action
verb	describes a noun
adjective	a person, place, or thing

1.10
a. verb
b. adjective
c. noun
d. verb
e. adjective
f. verb
g. noun
h. adjective

1.11 *Red* (*nouns*): baby, eye, garden, picture, shirt, sister, cow, pizza, bell, apple, paper, hill

Blue (*verbs*): dig, talk, see, add, jumped, blow, feed, look, give, learn, read, took

Green (*adjectives*): good, silly, grumpy, scary

1.12 Teacher check

1.13 Teacher check

1.14
a. cent
b. city
c. lace
d. slice
e. age
f. cage
g. gem
h. gym
i. cause
j. please
k. raise
l. does

1.15

1414 West Oak Street
Meadows, KS 23344
November 1, 20 ___

Dear Ruby,

I am glad that you got a new dog! I remember that you liked my dog Tippy. Remember the tricks that Tippy could do? Are you going to teach Pepper some tricks?

I asked my mom if we can visit you sometime. She said that maybe we can come next summer! That would be fun!

Your friend,
Anna

1.16 Teacher check

1.17 Any order within categories:

a. **Silent l**
calf
salmon
folk
walk

b. **Silent b**
numb
crumb
lamb
dumb
plumb

c. **Silent s**
loss
miss
moss
boss

d. **Silent gh**
night
sigh
bright
bought
might

1.18

a.	(right)	rit
b.	mes	(mess)
c.	(half)	haf
d.	dres	(dress)
e.	(chalk)	chak
f.	gras	(grass)
g.	(press)	pres
h.	(less)	les
i.	(fight)	fite
j.	(thumb)	thum
k.	(talk)	tak
l.	lam	(lamb)
m.	yok	(yolk)

Answer: read carefully

1.19 Teacher check

1.20
a. David's
b. Kelsey's
c. Anna's
d. Ruby's

1.21
a. the dog's dish
b. Andy's sandwich
c. Mother's oven
d. Ann's bike
e. Alex's clothes
f. Leah's friend

SELF TEST 1

1.01
a. laugh
b. rough
c. orphan
d. phone
e. tough

1.02
gem — jĕm
city — sĭtē
giraffe — jə-**răf**
please — plēz
cent — sĕnt

1.03 noun

1.04 verb

1.05 adjective

1.06
a. sign (g crossed out)
b. fight (gh crossed out)
c. mess (final s crossed out)
d. lamb (b crossed out)

1.07 ~~foot~~

1.08 Glen's

1.09 Jan's

1.010 puppy's

1.011 Dad's

1.012 lace

1.013 rice

SECTION 2

2.1 Possible answers:
- a. comb
- b. high
- c. loss, knew
- d. knife
- e. lamb
- f. light
- g. knew, loss
- h. mess
- i. might
- j. sigh
- k. sign
- l. wrap

2.2
- a. heading
- b. greeting
- c. body
- d. closing
- e. signature

2.3
- a. Street
- b. WA 67548
- c. June
- d. Greg
- e. Camp Sunshine
- f. canoe
- g. wet
- h. life
- i. Duke
- j. sad
- k. fun
- l. Uncle Ryan

2.4
- a. Answers will vary
- b. NJ
- c. FL
- d. Colorado
- e. Alaska

2.5 Teacher check

2.6 Greg Boyer
54 Apple Lane
Wonton, WA 67584

Ryan Van Sagten
4545 Oak Street
Atley, WA 67548

Teacher check

2.7

a. si**g**n	b. si**g**h	c. hi**g**h
d. li**g**ht	e. mi**g**ht	f. l**a**mb
g. c**o**mb	h. kn**e**w	i. kn**i**fe
j. wr**a**p	k. m**e**ss	l. l**o**ss

2.8

~~k~~nife	~~w~~rist	~~w~~hole	~~w~~rong
~~g~~nu	~~k~~nit	~~k~~neel	~~k~~nob
~~w~~ho	~~g~~nome	~~g~~naw	~~w~~rinkle
~~w~~rite	~~k~~not	r~~h~~ino	r~~h~~ubarb

2.9 See below:

a.	**kn**eel	☐ k	☑ n	☐ r
b.	**wh**o	☐ w	☐ r	☑ h
c.	**wr**ap	☑ r	☐ w	☐ h
d.	**rh**ino	☐ h	☑ r	☐ f
e.	**gn**u	☐ g	☑ n	☐ h
f.	**kn**ock	☐ k	☐ l	☑ n
g.	**wh**ole	☐ f	☐ w	☑ h
h.	**rh**yme	☑ r	☐ f	☐ h
i.	**wr**ist	☑ r	☐ w	☐ h
j.	**rh**ubarb	☑ r	☐ h	☐ f
k.	**gn**ome	☑ n	☐ g	☐ h

2.10
j
h
c
k
f
i
a
e
g
l
d
b

2.11

l	z	s	i	g	n	q	x	u	m	l
a	k	i	j	z	w	r	a	p	e	i
m	n	g	q	x	c	o	m	b	s	g
b	i	h	i	g	h	u	j	u	s	h
u	f	z	x	v	y	m	i	g	h	t
x	e	k	n	e	w	z	l	o	s	s

2.12
- a. rabbit's
- b. Sam's
- c. Clara's
- d. Jason's

2.13 a. Rachels crayons are broken.
Rachel's crayons are broken.
b. The cat ate from the dog's dish.
The cat ate from the dogs dish.
c. Brents bike has a flat tire.
Brent's bike has a flat tire.
d. The babys shoes are too small.
The baby's shoes are too small.

2.14 **Jennifer's Fishing Trip**
Jennifer went to her grandpa's house. They wanted to go fishing in the neighbor's pond. They rode in Grandpa's truck. Grandpa put Jennifer's fishing rod in the back of the truck. Grandpa's dog jumped into the truck. They caught many fish. The fish's scales gleamed brightly in the sun.

2.15 Suggested answer:
The possessive words have apostrophes in them.

2.16 a. Grandpa's house
b. the neighbor's pond
c. Grandpa's truck
d. Jennifer's fishing rod
e. Grandpa's dog
f. the fish's scales

2.17 Teacher check

2.18 Student answer – Teacher check

2.19 Teacher check

2.20 a. scared b. mail
c. neat d. jump
e. hurry f. drops
g. story h. build
i. friends j. fluffy
k. look l. wet

2.21 f
c
l
a
i
k
b
j
d
e
h
g

SELF TEST 2

2.01 a. heading
b. greeting
c. body
d. closing
e. signature

2.02 Sammy Pike
900 Lake Street
Plain, UT 12346

Levi Smith
1821 Park Avenue
Osborn, UT 12345

2.03 Sandy Van
3010 Fig Avenue
Rock River, IA 55113

2.04 a. com~~b~~ b. ~~k~~nee
c. ~~w~~rap d. r~~h~~yme
e. tos~~s~~

2.05 a. plural
b. possessive
c. plural
d. possessive

2.06 Paul

2.07 a. joyful
b. starving

2.08 a. bad
b. small

2.09

Florida	NY
New York	IA
Rhode Island	FL
Iowa	RI

(Florida – FL; New York – NY; Rhode Island – RI; Iowa – IA)

SECTION 3

3.1 Possible answers:
- a. know, here, hear, dear, deer
- b. dear, know, deer, here, hear
- c. deer, know, dear, here, hear
- d. here, hear, know, dear, deer
- e. weak, week
- f. week, weak
- g. hear, here, know, dear, deer
- h. no
- i. tail
- j. tale
- k. one, won
- l. won, one

3.2

Jessica and her family	was where they decided to go.
The state of Maine	was fun for the family.
There	went on a vacation.
The lighthouses	are on rocky shores.
Many pictures	are many lighthouses in Maine.
This vacation to Maine	were taken of the lighthouse.

3.3
- a. Jessica and her family went on a vacation.
- b. The state of Maine was where they decided to go.
- c. There are many lighthouses in Maine.
- d. The lighthouses are on rocky shores.
- e. Many pictures were taken of the lighthouse.
- f. This vacation to Maine was fun for the family.

3.4

Dear Angela,
I am having so much fun in Maine! I wish you were here! We swam in the Atlantic Ocean. We saw a big lighthouse. I will see you in a few days.
Your friend,
Jessica

Angela Swanson
7870 Curvy Drive
New York, NY 23456

3.5 l
h
f
a
i
k
c
j
d
e
b
g

3.6 a. know b. no
c. tail d. tale
e. dear f. deer
g. here h. hear
i. weak j. week
k. one l. won

3.7 – 3.10 Teacher check

3.11 Teacher check

3.12 Teacher check

3.13 a. aunt b. bee
c. by d. sell
e. you f. whole
g. I h. not
i. meet j. oar
k. pear l. write
m. see

3.14 bawl bear carrot deer
flower feet eye night

3.15 a. in b. sun
c. flowers d. would
e. see f. moose
g. two h. bears
i. berries j. paws
k. blue l. be

3.16 Teacher check

3.17 a. 3 b. 4 c. 5
d. 6 e. 7

3.18 Laundry Helpers – Teacher check

3.19 Teacher check

3.20

a. sine	sign
b. sity	city
c. lase	lace
d. tayle	tale
e. mite	might
f. kaje	cage
g. kome	comb
h. knoo	knew
i. cauze	cause
j. weke	week
k. mes	mess
l. duz	does

SELF TEST 3

3.01
- ☒ It was Tonya's birthday.
- ☐ Having a birthday party.
- ☒ All of her friends came to her house.
- ☐ Tonya and her friends.
- ☒ They sang "Happy Birthday" to Tonya.
- ☐ Blew out the candles on her cake.
- ☒ Tonya got many nice presents from her friends.

3.02 two
3.03 bare
3.04 dear
3.05 meat
3.06 – 3.09 Teacher check
3.010 sun
3.011 hear
3.012 ant
3.013 aunt
3.014 write
3.015 week

UNIT REVIEW

1.

2.

3.

knife	sigh	wrinkle	wrist
gnu	whole	rhubarb	rhyme
knee	kneel	wreck	crumb
who	gnaw	knight	salmon
mess	rhino	wreath	bright
knit	wrong	knob	plumb
gnome	knob	might	calf

4. (gh) zh jh (ph) th

5. c t (s) h v

6.

H	A
S	H
S	A
A	S
H	H

7.
a. 4
b. 5
c. 3
d. 2
e. 1

8. Paul

9.
- ☒ Nathan has a pen pal who lives in Spain.
- ☐ Gets letters every month.
- ☐ The name of Nathan's pen pal.
- ☒ Nathan hopes to visit his pen pal someday.

LIFEPAC TEST

1. footing
2. Kelly Jeena
   54 Western Street
   Silley, CO 97531

3.–6. Any order:

3. phone
4. cough
5. alphabet
6. laugh
7. s
8. z
9. s
10. z
11. s
12. z
13. a. calf b. sign c. lamb
    d. boss e. night f. walk
    g. knife h. wrap i. who
14. a
15. a
16. b
17. apples
18. cows
19. boys
20. cage — kāj
    fence — fĕns
    city — sĭtē
    please — plēz
    rice — rīs
21. bear
22. bare
23. weak
24. week
25. 4

ALTERNATE LIFEPAC TEST

1. neck
2. Cory Jameson
   1000 Lincoln Avenue
   Marvin, ID 86420
3. Any order:
   orphan
   tough
   gopher
   rough
4. z
5. s
6. s
7. z
8. s
9. z
10. folk
11. sign
12. comb
13. loss
14. light
15. talk
16. knee
17. write
18. who
19. b
20. a
21. b
22. puzzles
23. papers
24. kittens
25. city — sĭtē
    cage — kāj
    fence — fĕns
    please — plēz
    rice — rīs
26. write
27. right
28. knot
29. not
30. 2

SPELLING TEST

1	cent	A penny is worth one **cent**.	cent
2	loss	They mourned the **loss** of their pet.	loss
3	know	Do you **know** the answer to the riddle?	know
4	please	When you say **please**, you are using good manners.	please
5	lamb	The little **lamb** had soft fleece.	lamb
6	won	They **won** the basketball game by only one point.	won
7	city	Denver is a large **city**.	city
8	sign	There is a new **sign** on the mailbox.	sign
9	here	You are **here** taking a spelling test.	here
10	gem	A diamond is a very precious **gem**.	gem
11	wrap	Mother will **wrap** Grandmother's present.	wrap
12	deer	The **deer** was hiding in the woods.	deer
13	lace	The wedding gown had beautiful **lace**.	lace
14	light	The **light** bulb is burned out.	light
15	tail	The dog wagged its **tail** when it saw its master.	tail
16	cage	The lion was in a **cage** at the zoo.	cage
17	knife	Father carved the turkey with a very sharp **knife**.	knife
18	week	There are seven days in one **week**.	week
19	slice	There is only one **slice** of bread left.	slice
20	knew	He **knew** how to write in cursive.	knew

LANGUAGE ARTS 207

ALTERNATE LIFEPAC TEST

Name ______________________

Date ______________________

Each answer = 1 point

Circle the word that is *not* part of a friendly letter.

1. heading
greeting
neck
body
closing
signature

Write the address below in the correct order on the lines.

2. Cory Jameson ______________________
Marvin, ID 86420 ______________________
1000 Lincoln Avenue ______________________

Read the words below.
Write the four words that have the *f* sound on the lines.

orphan	tough	gopher	light
plate	night	height	rough

3. ____________________

____

____

____

Read the words.
Write *S* on the blank if the *s* makes an *s* sound.
Write *Z* on the blank if the *s* makes a *z* sound.

4. is ________ **5.** its ________ **6.** cats ________

7. words ________ **8.** horse ________ **9.** his ________

Read the words.
Put an X on the silent consonant in each word.

10. folk **11.** sign **12.** comb

13. loss **14.** light **15.** talk

16. knee **17.** write **18.** who

Read the sentences.
Put an X in the box that has the possessive noun written correctly.

19. a. ☐ Fathers' car needs to be washed.
b. ☐ Father's car needs to be washed.

20. a. ☐ Lacy mowed the neighbor's lawn.
b. ☐ Lacy mowed the neighbors' lawn.

21. a. ☐ Blakes' drawing won first place in the art contest.
b. ☐ Blake's drawing won first place in the art contest.

Circle the word in each sentence that is a plural noun.

22. Alyssa's brother likes to put puzzles together.

23. The teacher's papers fell on the floor.

24. The kittens in Grandpa's barn are scared of the dog.

Draw a line from the way the word is spelled to the way it is pronounced.

25.

city ▸	◂ plēz
cage ▸	◂ rīs
fence ▸	◂ kāj
please ▸	◂ fĕns
rice ▸	◂ sĭtē

Circle the homonym that correctly completes each sentence.

26. Beth will **write** **right** a letter to her sister.

27. Beth holds her pencil in her **write** **right** hand.

28. Colby has a **not** **knot** in his shoelace.

29. Austin will **not** **knot** eat his broccoli.

Read the story and answer the question below.

Farm Work

Josh and Jackie live on a farm. They need to wake up early to do their chores.

First, they have to feed the pigs. Then they brush their pet horse. Before they go back to the house, they gather the eggs.

30. How many paragraphs does this story have? __________

ALTERNATE SPELLING TEST

1	gym	We are going to the **gym** to play basketball.	gym
2	comb	Greg forgot to **comb** his hair before his picture was taken.	comb
3	weak	You will become **weak** if you do not eat.	weak
4	age	Sometimes cheese gets better (and more stinky) with **age**.	age
5	high	She put the baby in the **high** chair.	high
6	dear	You begin a friendly letter with the word **dear**.	dear
7	raise	Greg's dad got a **raise** in his pay at work.	raise
8	might	Father said that we **might** play softball after supper.	might
9	tale	Grandfather told a tall **tale** about a horse that could talk.	tale
10	cause	They do not know the **cause** of the fire.	cause
11	sigh	Sally gave a **sigh** of relief when she finished her math test.	sigh
12	no	There were **no** cookies left in the cookie jar.	no
13	does	Mark **does** not like lima beans.	does
14	mess	There was a muddy **mess** in the yard after the heavy rain.	mess
15	hear	Ann did not **hear** the phone ring.	hear
16	one	The softball team only scored **one** point.	one
17	cage	Kelly was upset when she found her bird was not in its **cage**.	cage
18	lamb	The little **lamb** followed its mother.	lamb
19	tail	That cat has a white tip on the end of its **tail**.	tail
20	slice	There was only one **slice** of pizza left.	slice

LANGUAGE ARTS 208

Unit 8: Pronouns

TEACHER NOTES

MATERIALS NEEDED FOR LIFEPAC	
Required	Suggested
• sharp pencil	• crayons or colored pencils • notebook or composition book for journaling • paper with guidelines for Spelling Tests

OPTIONAL ADDITIONAL LEARNING ACTIVITIES

The theme of this unit is to find the parts of a story: character, plot, and setting, and predicting. Also, cursive writing is introduced in this unit.

Section 1

1. Begin this unit by writing the following title on the board or a large piece of paper: "Beautiful Insects" (include a picture of a caterpillar and butterfly). Tell the students that you are going to read them a short article. The title of the article is "Beautiful Insects." Ask the students to predict what the article will be about. Show them the pictures of the caterpillar and butterfly. Explain to the students that the title of stories and pictures that go with the story can help us predict or guess what the story is going to be. Read the following article:

   Beautiful Insects

   The butterfly is a beautiful insect that God created. Their colorful wings help them fly gracefully.

   Butterflies can be found in most areas of the world. They can be found in jungles, deserts, and mountains. They are not found in areas that are cold most of the year.

   Have you seen a butterfly where you live? Some people say that you've been kissed by a butterfly if it lands on you! Did a butterfly ever land on you? Praise God for the beautiful butterfly!

2. Ask the students: What was the topic of this article? Did they predict correctly that this article would be about butterflies? Ask the students where butterflies can be found. Where are butterflies not found? What does it mean to be kissed by a butterfly?
3. Have the students color the butterfly picture. (Or make butterflies using tissue paper and pipe cleaners.)

Section 2

1. Read a short story to the students. Ask the students to identify the characters, setting, and plot.
2. Do some verbal analogies with the students; have the students complete these analogies:

   Eye is to see as ear is to _______ (hear).

Duck is to quack as cow is to _________ (moo).

Yellow is to sun as blue is to __________ (sky).

Glad is to happy as angry is to _________ (mad).

Sheep is to lamb as bear is to __________ (cub).

Earring is to ear as ring is to __________ (finger).

3. Say the following words with the students. Clap with the words to determine the amount of syllables each word has.

cake	button	food	basket
goat	apple	six	baby
map	pillow	spoon	ice
teacher	kitten	nose	tent

4. Have the students orally give you proper nouns for these common nouns:

state city lake girl boy

Section 3

1. Draw the word web to help the students think about details. Tell the students to think about a kitchen or tree (or the teacher can use another word for the word web of their choice). Have the students complete the word web.

Examples:

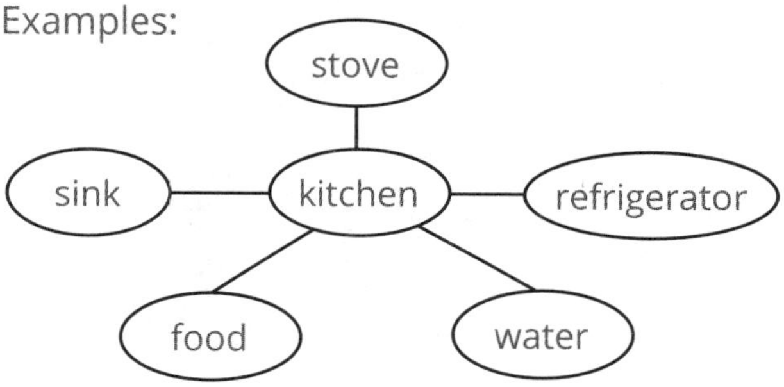

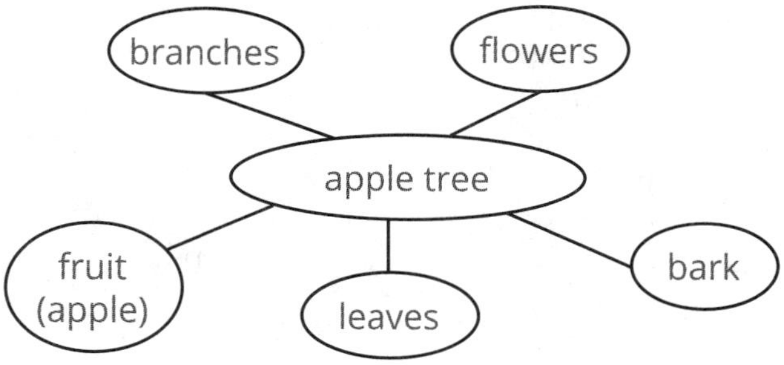

2. Review compound words with the students by thinking of compound words that have the word *ball*, such as: basketball, baseball, football, kickball, softball.

Suggested Books:

Animal Fact/Animal Fiction by Seymour Simon

Journal Suggestions:

After reading *Animal Fact/Animal Fiction*, have the students do some research about an animal and write their own animal fact/animal fiction (similar in style to the book).

Administer the LIFEPAC Spelling Test.

Administer the LIFEPAC Test.

ANSWER KEYS

SECTION 1

1.1 Possible answers:
a. scold, small
b. scrape
c. skate
d. small, scold
e. snap
f. split
g. spoon
h. spray
i. step
j. stray
k. swim
l. twin

1.2 Student answer – suggested answer: one of God's special creatures

1.3 Student answer – suggested answer: about spiders

1.4 Student answer

1.5 Student answer

1.6
a. beach
b. shells
c. lunch
d. peaches
e. boxes
f. jackets

1.7
a. brushed   b balloons
c. eggs   d glasses
e. boxes   f. wishes
g. watches   h papers
i. dresses   j. buses
k. taxes   l. flags
m. wheels   n branches

1.8
a. use**ful** useful   b rest**ful** restful
c. cheer**ful** cheerful   d play**ful** playful

1.9
a. wonderful
b. sinful
c. fearful
d. hopeful

1.10
a. careful   b forgetful
c. delightful   d frightful
e. painful   f. sorrowful
g. truthful   h harmful
i. graceful   j. helpful
k. wonderful   l. joyful

1.11
a. scold
b. scrape
c. skate
d. small
e. snap
f. split
g. spoon
h. spray
i. step
j. stray
k. swim
l. twin

1.12
a. The boy lived in the city with a dog and cat.
b. The dog ran after the cat.
c. The cat went up a tree.
d. The tree was near a street.
e. The boy asked his dad for help.
f. The boy and his dad got the cat from the tree.

1.13
a. Dave lived in Denver with Spot and Fluffy.
b. Spot ran after Fluffy.
c. Fluffy went up a tree.
d. The tree was near Oak Street.
e. Dave asked his dad for help.
f. Dave and his dad got Fluffy from the tree.

1.14
a. Dave lived in Denver with Spot and Fluffy.
b. Spot ran after Fluffy.
c. Fluffy went up a tree.
d. The tree was near Oak Street.
e. Dave asked his dad for help.
f. Dad got Fluffy from the tree.

1.15
a. Dave lived in Denver with Spot and Fluffy.
b. Spot ran after Fluffy.
c. Fluffy went up a tree.
d. The tree was near Oak Street.
e. Dave asked his dad for help.
f. Dad got Fluffy from the tree.

1.16
a. scold   b. spray
c. scrape   d. stray
e. small   f. split
g. skate   h. step
i. snap   j. spoon
k. swim   l. twin

1.17 a. 1
b. 2
c. 1
d. 1
e. 2

1.18 Suggested answers:
a. He needed a haircut.
b. Jon went to the barber.
c. Jon's dad took him to the barber.
d. Jon sat on a special chair.
e. The barber put a cape on Jon.

1.19 The barber will cut Jon's hair.

1.20 a. The barber cut Jon's hair with clippers.
b. Student answer.
c. Student answer.

1.21 a. kitchen b. church
c. gym d. barn
e. bedroom

1.22 a. Dogs are good pets.
b. Riding a bike is fun.
c. It was a rainy day.
d. The clown was funny.

1.23 Teacher check

1.24 a. useless
b. sleepless
c. harmless
d. fearless
e. thickness
f. darkness
g. kindness
h. goodness

1.25 Circled words: gentleness, goodness, meekness.

1.26 gentle good meek

1.27 a. breathless
b. careless
c. regardless
d. hopeless
e. endless
f. speechless

1.28 a. lovely b. greatly
c. loudly d. partly
e. nightly f. bravely
g. slowly h. nearly

1.29 a. fresh(ly) fresh
b. dai(ly) day
c. cost(ly) cost
d. kind(ly) kind

1.30 Teacher check

SELF TEST 1

1.01

characters	the people in a story
predict	to guess about a story by reading the title and looking at the pictures
artist	someone who illustrates a story
plot	what happens in a story
author	someone who writes a story
dialogue	what the characters say in a story
setting	where a story takes place
intent	the author's reason for writing

1.02 Any order: airplane, sister, turns

1.03 Either order: Luke, Jessica

1.04 Any order: bought, likes, is, helps, take

1.05

c	f	l	y	d	a	r	t
z	o	o	m	s	o	a	r
r	i	s	e	r	z	i	p
a	g	l	i	d	e	s	h

Circled: fly, dart, zoom, soar, rise, zip, glide

1.06 crash

1.07 2

1.08 1

1.09 a. carrot~~s~~ b. radish~~es~~ c. help~~ful~~
d. dish~~es~~ e. light~~ly~~ f. care~~less~~
g. good~~ness~~ h. sad~~ly~~ i. help~~less~~

SECTION 2

2.1 Possible answers:
- a. sung, sing
- b. bang, fang, long
- c. lodge, fudge, badge, ledge
- d. fudge, lodge, badge, ledge
- e. fang, bang, long
- f. edge
- g. ridge
- h. long, bang, fang
- i. thing
- j. ledge, badge, lodge, fudge
- k. badge, ledge, lodge, fudge
- l. sing, sung

2.2
- a. boy
- b. dog
- c. cat
- d. tree
- e. boy
- f. boy dad cat

2.3 Hi. My name is Meg. I have a puppy named Baxter. He is a puppy that likes to eat. Sometimes he eats six bowls of dog food a day!

Baxter sleeps in a little doghouse. Soon he will not be able to fit in it. I think he should sleep in the laundry room. Mother does not want Baxter in the laundry room. She thinks he could make a big mess there.

Father and Mother think Baxter should sleep in the garage. They think that would be a good place for a dog.

Someday we will have to find a bigger sleeping place for Baxter!

2.4
- a. He
- b. him
- c. she, them
- d. They
- e. him

2.5 Suggested answers:
- a. Joe and Mike
- b. Joe lives in a small town and likes to do things with Mike
- c. in a small town called Allen

2.6
- a. Pine Street
- b. Elm Street
- c. the library
- d. Mike
- e. swings, teeter-totter, slides, merry-go-round
- f. get an ice cream cone
- g. Pine Street
Oak Street

2.7 Teacher check

2.8
- a. playing
- b. jumping
- c. turning
- d. waiting
- e. throwing

2.9
- a. opened b. wanted
- c. helped d. locked
- e. played f. looked

2.10
- a. wanted
- b. locked
- c. looked
- d. helped
- e. opened
- f. played

2.11
- a. fix b. walk
- c. laugh d. paint
- e. jump f. talk
- g. pass h. point
- i. clean j. work

2.12
- a. floated floating
- b. talked talking
- c. cheered cheering
- d. followed following
- e. prayed praying
- f. crawled crawling
- g. cooked cooking
- h. climbed climbing

2.13
- a. walking
- b. walked
- c. following
- d. followed
- e. jumping
- f. jumped
- g. watched
- h. watching
- i. laughed
- j. laughing
- k. talking
- l. talked

2.14
- a. begged begging
- b. chatted chatting
- c. gripped gripping
- d. hopped hopping
- e. jogged jogging
- f. napped napping
- g. planned planning
- h. shopped shopping
- i. slipped slipping
- j. snapped snapping
- k. trotted trotting
- l. tugged tugging

2.15
a. rubbed — rubbing
b. framed — framing
c. hugged — hugging
d. poked — poking

2.16
a. fished
b. fishing
c. looked
d. looking
e. hoping
f. hoped
g. tugging
h. tugged
i. flopping
j. flopped
k. slipped
l. slipping

2.17
a. bang — fang
b. sung
c. sing — thing
d. edge — ledge
e. fudge
f. long
g. ridge
h. lodge
i. badge

2.18

n	z	s	h	e	y
o	I	u	s	t	i
y	o	u	j	h	t
g	f	k	h	e	w
t	h	e	y	m	e

2.19 Any order:
she
I
us
you
he
they
me
them
it
we

2.20 Alphabetical Order:
he
I
it
me
she
them
they
us
we
you

2.21 **Jesus and Friends**

Jesus had many friends. He had twelve men that were special friends. They were called disciples. They helped Jesus.

Mary and Martha were friends of Jesus. They were sisters. Jesus had many meals with them. Martha was a good worker. She liked to cook. Mary was a good listener. She liked to hear what Jesus had to say. Sometimes Martha worked while Jesus was talking to Mary. Jesus told Martha that sometimes it is better to listen than to work.

Now you know about some of the friends of Jesus. I know Jesus is a special friend to me. He loves me. He loves you. He loves us. We can be glad Jesus is our friend.

Note: The word "our" in the story is a pronoun, but it hasn't been taught to the students.

2.22 Teacher check

2.23
a. The Mighty Mississippi
b. Trips to Washington, D.C.
c. My Pet Horse, Ginger
d. On the Trail with Ginger

2.24 Teacher check

2.25 Teacher check

SELF TEST 2

2.01 a. holding
b. writing
c. staying
d. chasing
e. reading
f. stopping

2.02 a. started
b. helped
c. hoped
d. fished
e. chopped
f. loved

2.03 a. Debbie, Grandma, Mom
b. Grandma and Debbie bake a birthday cake.
c. Grandma's kitchen
d. A Surprise for Mom

2.04 a. they
b. it
c. she
d. them, she

2.05 a. skated
b. skates
c. chased
d. hissed

SECTION 3

3.1 Possible answers:
a. bleach
b. church
c. skunk, stand, stink, clock
d. snack, crash
e. grind
f. stand, skunk, stink, clock
g. crash, snack
h. stink, skunk, stand, clock
i. clock, skunk, stand, stink
j. thick
k. truck
l. truth

3.2 a. short
b. cry
c. messy
d. sad

3.3 a. grass
b. hear
c. farm
d. kitten
e. cold

3.4 cat chick bird frog skunk
dog pig bat fox wolf

3.5 deer bee dove goat seal
toad sheep ape hare whale

3.6 j
b
k
g
e
c
a
d
h
f
i
l

3.7 a. fact b. fiction

3.8 e s i u r w t
w r u t s i e

3.9 it we tie wet
tie it we wet

3.10 Teacher check

3.11 See below:

g	z	s	x	a	t	r	u	c	k	y	b	q	s
r	s	t	r	u	t	h	f	u	s	n	a	c	k
i	t	i	j	v	b	l	e	a	c	h	w	l	u
n	a	n	xh	z	k	c	h	u	r	c	h	o	n
d	n	k	z	g	f	o	u	l	t	r	b	c	k
v	d	x	c	r	a	s	h	g	k	p	l	k	z
q	d	w	t	h	i	c	k	v	x	d	d	h	s

3.12 a. 2 b. 1 c. 1 d. 1
e. 1 f. 1 g. 1 h. 2
i. 2 j. 1 k. 2 l. 1

3.13 Teacher check

3.14 Hope spilled her milk. — Barry had to play inside.
It rained all day long. — They built a sandcastle.
Abigail's pencil broke. — The cat lapped up the milk.
The family traveled to the beach. — She could not write.

3.15 Teacher check

3.16 f — *b*
b — *f*
l — *h*
k — *l*
h — *k*

3.17 Teacher check

3.18 See below

~~skaet~~	snap	~~skold~~	edge	~~lege~~	badge
~~swimm~~	step	small	~~fudje~~	~~loge~~	ridge
scrape	twin	~~spoun~~	~~snak~~	church	skunk

stray	~~sprai~~	~~splite~~	~~stadn~~	~~thik~~	grind
~~bange~~	fang	sung	~~truk~~	stink	crash
sing	~~logn~~	thing	truth	bleach	~~klok~~

SELF TEST 3

3.01 car
3.02 toe
3.03 fruit
3.04 cub
3.05 head
3.06 fiction
3.07 fact
3.08 fiction
3.09 1
3.010 1
3.011 2
3.012 2
3.013 1
3.014 1
3.015 Rachel visited her grandma. — The dog hid under the bed.
3.016 The thunder was loud. — Her grandma was happy.
3.017 Stacy went to the library. — Many apple trees grew.
3.018 Johnny Appleseed planted apple seeds. — She checked out a book about frogs.

UNIT REVIEW

1. d
2. f
3. b
4. g
5. a
6. h
7. e
8. c
9. Alex
10. Any order:
aquarium, zoo, fish, books, pictures, money, store
11. Any order:
like, swim, read, drew, wanted, told, needed, saved, earned, took, helped
12. Any order: he, they, it, she
13. An Aquarium for Alex
14. (Alex) Amber (Mother) Grandmother (Father)
15. Alex likes aquariums and gets one of his own.
16. at Alex's home, the zoo, and the pet store
17.

lik(ed)	like	talk(ing)	talk
want(ed)	want	read(ing)	read
sav(ed)	save	watch(es)	watch
hopp(ed)	hop	help(s)	help
swimm(ing)	swim	need(s)	need
tell(ing)	tell	draw(s)	draw

18. Duck for President! Cinder-Rabbit
19. money
20. needle
21.

Eve left the ice cream out on the counter.	She saw lots of animals.
Gina went to the zoo.	It melted and made a mess.

(Eve left the ice cream out on the counter. — It melted and made a mess.; Gina went to the zoo. — She saw lots of animals.)

22. Teacher check

LIFEPAC TEST

1. characters
2. plot
3. setting
4. 2
5. Any order:
sky, apple, penny, arm
6. Any order:
Aaron, Texas, Denver, Oak Lake
7. Any order:
ask, eat, tell, see
8. Any order:
they, he, you, it
9. a. sweetly b. useful
c. careless d. reads
e. chopped f. swimming
10. Rick went to church on Sunday.
He learned about Jesus.
11. Jessica forgot to set her alarm clock.
She woke up late.
12. We are out of bread.
We went to the grocery store.
13. fruit
14. lamb
15. cut
16. Click, Clack, Moo—Cows That Type
17.

e	*w*	r	*k*
s	*i*	f	*l*
i	*u*	b	*r*
u	*e*	l	*f*
w	*s*	k	*b*
t	*t*		

(Each printed letter is matched to the same letter in cursive.)

ALTERNATE LIFEPAC TEST

1. a. plot
b. characters
c. setting

2. 2

3. Nouns – Any order:
dime, leg, earth, pear

4. Proper Nouns – Any order:
Lucas, Utah, Dallas, Red Sea

5. Verbs – Any order:
create, speak, teach, seek

6. Pronouns – Any order:
I, we, she, me

7.

a. quick~~ly~~	quick
b. care~~ful~~	care
c. use~~less~~	use
d. writi~~ng~~	write
e. jump~~ed~~	jump
f. watch~~es~~	watch

8.

Leah put on her stocking cap.	He is tired today.
Kaden studied for his spelling test.	He got a good grade.
Bernie stayed up late last night.	Her head stayed warm.

9. glove

10. car

11. shut

12. Cat in the Hat

13.

k	w
l	k
u	u
s	l
w	s

SPELLING TEST

1	small	Aunt Linda has a **small** house.	small
2	sing	Kristi likes to **sing** in the shower.	sing
3	skunk	You do not want to scare a **skunk**!	skunk
4	swim	Jordan likes to **swim** in the lake in the morning.	swim
5	badge	The police officer wears a shiny **badge**.	badge
6	snack	Our afternoon **snack** was apple slices with peanut butter.	snack
7	skate	Do you know how to **skate** backwards?	skate
8	fang	A **fang** is a long, pointed tooth.	fang
9	crash	The **crash** of thunder woke the baby.	crash
10	spray	Mom will **spray** water on the flower bed.	spray
11	lodge	My uncle has a **lodge** in the mountains.	lodge
12	truck	The farmer used his **truck** to bring the fruit to town.	truck
13	snap	Do you know how to **snap** your fingers?	snap
14	bang	The firecracker went off with a loud **bang**.	bang
15	clock	The **clock** in the kitchen needs a new battery.	clock
16	twin	Ellie has a **twin** sister named Mia.	twin
17	long	Josh got first place in the **long** jump.	long
18	church	It is important to go to **church**.	church
19	spoon	You should use a **spoon** instead of a fork to eat soup.	spoon
20	thing	It is a good **thing** to give thanks unto the Lord.	thing

LANGUAGE ARTS 208

ALTERNATE LIFEPAC TEST

Name ______________________

Date ______________________

Each answer = 1 point

Read the words below.
Write each word next to the correct definition.

characters	plot	setting

1. a. what happens in a story

____

b. the people or animals in a story

____

c. when or where a story takes place

____

Look at the pictures. Circle the *number* of the picture that shows what you predict will happen next.

2. 

1

2

Read the words below. Sort them into their correct categories.

Lucas	I	seek	Utah	she	earth
pear	teach	dime	create	we	leg
speak	Dallas	Red Sea	me		

3. Common Nouns:

____

____

____

____

4. Proper Nouns:

____

____

____

____

5. Verbs:

____

____

____

____

6. Pronouns:

____

____

____

____

Read the words.
Put an X on each suffix, and write the root word on the line.

7. a. quickly ______________
b. careful ______________
c. useless ______________
d. writing ______________
e. jumped ______________
f. watches ______________

Match the cause with the effect.

8.

Leah put on her stocking cap. ▸		◂ He is tired today.
Kaden studied for his spelling test. ▸		◂ He got a good grade.
Bernie stayed up late last night. ▸		◂ Her head stayed warm.

Write the word on the line that correctly completes the analogy.

9. Foot is to shoe as hand is to ______________________ .
(arm / glove)

10. Branch is to tree as wheel is to ______________________ .
(car / round)

11. Up is to down as open is to ______________________ .
(shut / left)

Complete this activity.

12. Mitch wants to buy a fiction book from the bookstore.
Read the titles of the books he is looking for.
Circle the title you predict will be a fiction book.

Cat in the Hat

Quakes

Stars

Draw a line from the manuscript letter to the cursive letter.

13.

Manuscript	Cursive
k ▸	◂ *w*
l ▸	◂ *k*
u ▸	◂ *u*
s ▸	◂ *l*
w ▸	◂ *s*

ALTERNATE SPELLING TEST

1	stand	Can you **stand** on your head?	stand
2	stray	Mike found a **stray** puppy in the park.	stray
3	sung	I have **sung** "Jesus Loves Me" many times in Sunday School.	sung
4	thick	Randy had a **thick** slice of ham on his sandwich.	thick
5	scold	Mother will **scold** you if you keep the fridge door open!	scold
6	edge	Annie was so excited she sat on the **edge** of her seat.	edge
7	grind	Father will **grind** the coffee for breakfast.	grind
8	scrape	**Scrape** the mud off your shoes before you come in the house.	scrape
9	fudge	Pam's favorite dessert is a hot **fudge** sundae.	fudge
10	truth	God wants us to always tell the **truth**.	truth
11	step	The baby took his first **step** yesterday.	step
12	ledge	The bird was sitting on the window **ledge**.	ledge
13	stink	A skunk can really **stink**!	stink
14	split	Grandpa will **split** the logs into firewood.	split
15	bleach	Alice used **bleach** to remove the stain on her blouse.	bleach
16	ridge	The sun was coming up over the **ridge** of the mountains.	ridge
17	swim	It is fun to **swim** on a hot day.	swim
18	sing	It is good to **sing** praises to the Lord!	sing
19	snack	Carrots are a healthy **snack**.	snack
20	small	A mouse is a **small** animal.	small

LANGUAGE ARTS 209

Unit 9: Verb Types and Tenses

TEACHER NOTES

MATERIALS NEEDED FOR LIFEPAC	
Required	Suggested
• sharp pencil	• crayons or colored pencils • notebook or composition book for journaling • paper with guidelines for Spelling Tests

OPTIONAL ADDITIONAL LEARNING ACTIVITIES

This unit introduces the students to reading different material other than books. Students will read menus, maps, road signs, and a pretend telephone directory. You can introduce students to reading food packages, closed caption of movies, appropriate children's magazines, store signs, newspapers, catalogs, church bulletins etc.

Section 1

1. Dictionary use: have the students write a word from the dictionary for every letter from the alphabet. See who comes up with the most interesting words!
2. Unusual sayings: sometimes people say some words that have a special meaning.
   Pretend that you broke a window in your house. Then your mother could say that you would be in "hot water." This doesn't really mean that you are in hot water, but that you are in BIG trouble. Can you guess what this saying means? — "Keep your fingers crossed."
   If you guessed that you hope your wish comes true, you are correct!
3. Can you match these sayings with their meanings?

Back to the drawing board	Eat a lot
Cold feet	Change for the better
Eaten out of house and home	Start a project over again
Turn over a new leaf	Become scared

Section 2

1. Make copies of an appropriate news or magazine article. Have the students underline or highlight the nouns in the article. The students may also circle the *be* verbs—are, is, was, and were—in the article.

Section 3

1. Dictionary use—Have the students find how to divide into syllables the following words by finding the words in the dictionary:

   garden   towel   funny   zebra   butterfly
2. Look at a seed catalog and make a pretend order.

Administer the LIFEPAC Spelling Test. / Administer the LIFEPAC Test.

ANSWER KEYS

SECTION 1

1.1 Suggested answers:
a. She hopped out of bed.
b. Her room had a window.
c. She put on her clothes (*or* robe).
d. She saw snow.
e. mittens (*or* gloves), boots, coat, scarf, hat

1.2
a. nose b. snow
c. bed d. cap (*or* hat)
e. coat f. scarf
g. mittens h. stones
i. wings j. window
k. snowman l. camera
m. carrot n. angel
o. twigs p. boots

1.3 A Fun Winter Day
1.4 Kristen's mother, Kristen
1.5 Kristen makes a snow angel and a snowman.
1.6 at Kristen's house in the winter
1.7 Teacher check
1.8 Possible answers:
a. lady
b. very, many
c. rainy
d. pinky
e. pull
f. off
g. ruby
h. sandy, rusty
i. use
j. rusty, sandy
k. many, very
l. work

1.9
a. bulldog
b. cupcake
c. landlord

1.10
a. her / self
b. pan / cake
c. shoe / lace
d. sail / boat
e. scare / crow
f. pop / corn

1.11
a. blossom
b. dollar
c. matter

1.12
a. bob / bin
b. fol / low
c. gal / lop
d. ham / mer
e. lad / der
f. mam / mal
g. mit / ten
h. pup / pet
i. sin / ner
j. soc / cer
k. tun / nel
l. zip / per

1.13
a. wor / ry
b. jel / ly
c. bag / gy
d. fol / ly
e. jif / fy
f. slop / py
g. pup / py

1.14 Any order within categories:

a.	b.
off	lady
use	ruby
pull	many
work	rusty
	sandy
	pinky
	very
	rainy

1.15
a. shone
b. took
c. wore
d. brought
e. flew
f. made
g. ate
h. felt
i. played
j. slept

1.16
a. add
b. bring
c. chew
d. decide
e. eat
f. fix
g. go
h. hurt
i. imagine

1.17 Teacher check

1.18 Suggested answers:
- a. It is a large glass of fresh, white whole milk.
- b. The five vegetables are radishes, broccoli, cauliflower, carrots, and celery.
- c. Student Answer
- d. Splendid Spaghetti is the most expensive meal.
- e. A glass of water is free.

1.19 Teacher check

1.20 Teacher check

1.21
- a. bas / ket
- b. fin / ger
- c. gar / den
- d. par / don
- e. bap / tize
- f. pic / nic

1.22
- a. le
- b. 2

1.23 It rained and rained. There was a large puddle in the front yard. Scott went outside. He threw a pebble in the water. He was surprised to see a little turtle walk by his ankle. Scott picked up the critter. It tried to wiggle out of Scott's hand. Scott started to giggle. Scott couldn't wait to show his Uncle Loren how he could handle this new, simple friend.

a. pud / dle	b. peb / ble
c. lit / tle	d. tur / tle
e. an / kle	f. wig / gle
g. gig / gle	h. Un / cle
i. han / dle	j. sim / ple

1.24 Teacher check

1.25 Any order: are, is, was, were

1.26

a. was	b. are
c. are	d. is
e. was	f. were

1.27
- a. ~~Clark and Candy was Jason's pet dogs.~~
- b. ~~The dogs was cute little puppies at one time.~~
- c. ~~They is now big dogs.~~
- d. ~~Clark were a silly dog.~~
- e. ~~Candy were smaller than Clark.~~
- f. ~~Both dogs is noisy.~~

1.28 a.

he is	we are	they was	they are
we was	they is	she are	she was
she is	I is	we is	they were

b.

Chris were	James was	Jo is	Jean are
the boys are	the boys is	the boys was	the boys were
the dog is	the dog was	the dogs are	the dogs were

1.29
- a. be
- b. be
- c. action
- d. action
- e. be
- f. action
- g. be

SELF TEST 1

1.01 Suggested answers:
menu, phone book

1.02 My family went to the beach.

1.03 My little brother built a sand castle.

1.04 Molly rode her bike.

1.05 The tired children went to bed early.

1.06 I played with my best friend Mike.

1.07 We liked going to the beach.

1.08

earth	ball
foot	ground
play	mill
up	stairs
wind	worm

1.09

a. 1	b. 1
c. 2	d. 2
e. 2	f. 1
g. 2	h. 1

1.010

a. din / ner	b. par / ty
c. tur / tle	d. bag / gy
e. dan / ger	f. zip / per
g. cor / ner	h. blos / som
i. tun / nel	j. gar / den
k. ap / ple	l. thim / ble

1.011 B

1.012 A

1.013 B

SECTION 2

2.1 Possible answers:
a. kitten, button, fellow, batter
b. dinner, borrow
c. button, kitten, fellow, batter
d. borrow, dinner
e. fellow, kitten, button, batter
f. batter, kitten, button, fellow
g. manner, narrow
h. muffin
i. narrow, manner
j. parrot
k. rugged
l. yellow

2.2 Suggested answers:
a. Pine Valley
b. 30 (mph)
c. Gil's Gas Station
d. turn left at the stop sign
e. Delicious Diner
f. 2 miles
g. Happy Hotel
h. on Main Street
i. Ohio

2.3 bicycle path

railroad crossing

curvy road ahead

hospital

no left turn

highway number

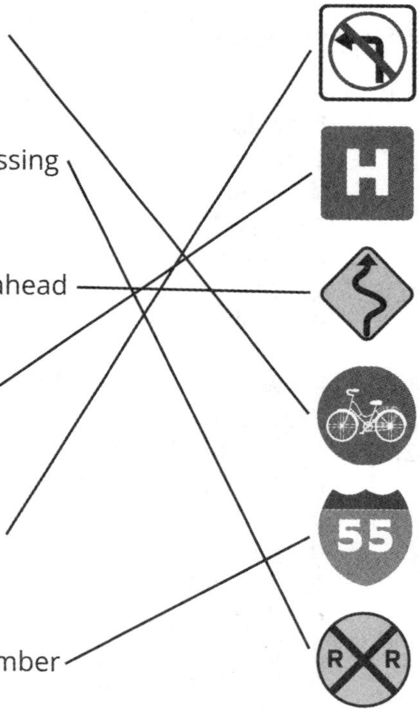

2.4

a. kit**ten**	b. din**ner**	c. bor**row**
d. but**ton**	e. fel**low**	f. rug**ged**
g. nar**row**	h. yel**low**	i. par**rot**
j. muf**fin**	k. man**ner**	l. bat**ter**

2.5
a. 5
b. Any order:
soil, sold, song, sop, soup
c. 9
d. Any order:
sofa, software, soggy, solar, sonar, sonic, sonnet, sorrow, soybean
e. software, soybean
f. 3
soggy, sonnet, sorrow
g. Any order:
sofa, software, soil, sonar, song, sonnet, sorrow, soup, soybean
h. sold, sop
i. soggy, solar, sonic

2.6
a. batter b. borrow
c. button d. dinner
e. fellow f. kitten
g. manner h. muffin
i. narrow j. parrot
k. rugged l. yellow

2.7
a. floated
b. licked
c. pack
d. moved

2.8
a. began
b. gave

2.9
a. wrote
b. colored
c. read
d. liked
e. told
f. made
g. kept
h. took
i. showed
j. want

2.10 Teacher check

2.11
a. (555) 345-6785
b. 1677 12th Street
c. 2
d. James Morris
e. Ben Stevens
f. (555) 345-3773
g. 2
h. (555) 345-1918
i. 3000 Easter Ave.
j. (555) 345-4746
k. 4
l. 26

2.12 Teacher check

2.13 Teacher check

2.14
rerun — to run again
refill — to fill again
rewire — to wire again
rewrite — to write again
replay — to play back
reheat — to heat again

2.15
a. run b. fill
c. wire d. write
e. play f. heat

2.16
a. Annie had to retake her school picture.
b. Jimmy had to redo his spelling test.
c. Mother had to reorder the car part.
d. Jimmy had to repay the money he owed to Tim.

2.17
a. unplug
b. unpack
c. undo
d. uneasy
e. unfit
f. unclean

2.18
a. unhappy
b. unclear
c. unfair
d. unable
e. uncover
f. unlock
g. unfold
h. unload

SELF TEST 2

2.01 d
2.02 b
2.03 a
2.04 g
2.05 e
2.06 f
2.07 c
2.08 1
2.09 a. cellar
b. cello
c. census
2.010 b
2.011 a
2.012 a
2.013 a
2.014 last name first, in alphabetical order
2.015 rerun — run again
rewrite — write again
unhappy — not happy
unload — opposite of load

2.016

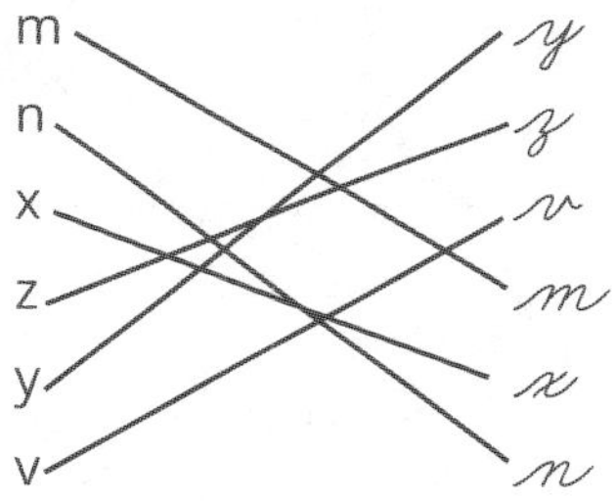

SECTION 3

3.1 Possible answers:
a. sister, number, center, wonder, mister
b. donkey
c. hermit
d. lumber
e. number, sister, center, wonder, mister
f. napkin
g. mister, sister, number, center, wonder
h. parcel
i. person
j. pester
k. center, wonder, number, sister, mister
l. wonder, center, number, sister, mister

3.2 a. Alyssa will go to the library.
b. She will get some books.
c. She will read the books.
d. Alyssa will walk home.

3.3 a. will bake
b. will enjoy
c. will go
d. will do
e. will visit

3.4 a. past
b. past
c. past
d. present
e. present
f. present
g. future
h. future
i. future

3.5 a. played
b. play
c. will play
d. baked
e. bake
f. will bake
g. saw
h. see
i. will see

3.6 a. cen / ter
b. don / key
c. her / mit
d. lum / ber
e. mis / ter
f. nap / kin
g. num / ber
h. par / cel
i. per / son
j. pes / ter
k. sis / ter
l. won / der

3.7 a. The dog barks loudly.
b. Kim and Joe laugh at the joke.
c. Jordan plays tennis with Jon.
d. The horse and donkey run fast.

3.8 a. grow
b. likes
c. eat
d. drinks
e. run
f. runs

3.9 a. center b. donkey
c. hermit d. lumber
e. mister f. number
g. napkin h. parcel
i. person j. pester
k. sister l. wonder

3.10 a. play b. skill
c. friend d. law

3.11 a. calm b. fair
c. igloo d. lady
e. odor f. rich
g. umbrella h. x-ray
i. zipper j. vain
k. think l. pepper
m. nice n. joke
o. help p. dog
q. braid r. add
s. eat t. glass
u. kick v. make
w. quick x. sad
y. wind z. yank

3.12 Teacher check

3.13 a. Mia drank milk, and Eli drank juice.
b. The dog chased the cat, and the cat chased the rat.
c. Tom drove a truck, and Cory drove a car.
d. Rachel likes to shop, and Beth likes to stay home.

3.14 a. Tim's favorite sport is basketball, **and h**is favorite basketball player is Kevin Garnett.
b. Sally goes to bed at 9 o'clock, **and s**he wakes up at 8 o'clock.
c. The cow stays in the barn, **and t**he chickens stay in the hay mow.
d. Leon likes to go fishing, **and h**is favorite fishing spot is a secret.

3.15 Teacher check

3.16

a	*g*
d	*o*
g	*q*
q	*a*
o	*c*
c	*d*

3.17

go	*dad*
add	*do*
do	*quit*
dad	*add*
dog	*go*
cod	*dog*
quit	*cod*

3.18 Teacher check

3.19 Spelling Review:

lady	kiten	sister
rainy	dinnur	number
pinky	senter	borrow
buttun	donkee	sandey
mister	felloe	rusty
ruby	ruged	napkin
very	narroe	wonder
yellow	maney	person
off	pesther	parrot
muffin	pul	lumber
use	maner	hermit
work	parsel	batter

Any order:
kitten button batter

SELF TEST 3

3.01 a. present
b. future
c. past

3.02 a. shines
b. need
c. drinks
d. needs
e. play

3.03 a. play   b. blow
c. grace   d. fit
e. take   f. help

3.04

reread	write again
unclear	not able
rewrite	read again
unable	opposite of clear

3.05 a
3.06 b
3.07 b

3.08 a
d
g
q
o
c

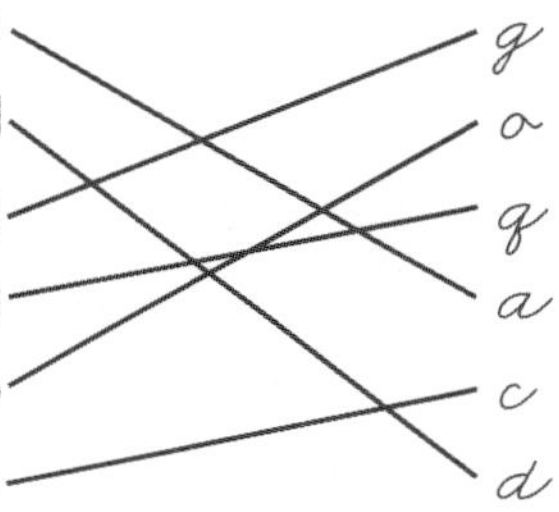

UNIT REVIEW

1. a. des / sert   b. ser / mon
c. out / fit   d. wal / nut
e. won / der   f. waf / fle
g. door / knob   h. hel / met
i. bull / dog

2. d
f
a
b
g
h
c
e

3. build   feel
call   play
easy   sleep
even   wish

4. was, is, are, were

5. jellyfish, cupcake, tiptoe

6. a. The fish swim in the lake, and the ducks float on the lake.
b. The dog chased the squirrel, and the squirrel ran up the tree.
c. The roosters crowed, and the hens laid eggs.
d. The penguins waddled across the ice, and the polar bear hunted for fish.

7. Any order within categories:

Past Tense	Present Tense	Future Tense
climbed	climb	will climb
filled	fill	will fill
tickled	tickle	will tickle
helped	help	will help
hugged	hugs	will hug
kicked	kicks	will kick
played	play	will play
saved	saves	will save

8. Ducks waddle around the pond.
Rabbits hop all around.
The eagle soars high in the sky.

9. Teacher check

LIFEPAC TEST

1.

air	self
her	boat
post	port
sail	card

2. See below:

bring	have	~~was~~	add	went	~~were~~
obey	sleep	fix	think	see	wobble
listen	~~is~~	eat	~~are~~	made	join
believe	had	follow	cut	think	climb

Any order: was, were, is, are

3. a. en / ter b. per / fect
c. pan / sy d. wil / low
e. in / to f. win / ner
g. sim / ple h. bam / boo

4. 1

5. a. napkin
b. narrate
c. naval

6. rewrite
7. unhappy
8. unload
9. rerun
10. future
11. past
12. present
13. law
14. even
15. talk
16. new
17. like
18. lives
19. plays
20. a
21. b
22. b
23.

a	*g*	n	*y*
d	*o*	v	*x*
g	*q*	x	*z*
q	*a*	y	*m*
o	*c*	z	*n*
c	*d*	m	*v*

ALTERNATE LIFEPAC TEST

1.

jelly	sand
fire	crow
quick	place
scare	fish

2. Any order:
a. are b. is
c. was d. were

3. a. hor / net b. per / cent
c. can / dy d. pil / low
e. may / be f. ban / ner
g. tur / tle h. den / tal

4. 2

5. Either order:
a. filly b. filthy

6. rebuild
7. uneven
8. uncover
9. redo
10. past
11. present
12. future
13. sing
14. swings
15. plays
16. hope
17. friend
18. turn
19. tie
20. jump
21. b
22. b
23. a
24.

n	*y*
g	*o*
y	*n*
o	*c*
c	*g*

SPELLING TEST

1	sister	My **sister** is scared of spiders.	sister
2	kitten	Elizabeth saw a cute **kitten** in the pet store.	kitten
3	rainy	It was a **rainy** day so the children played inside.	rainy
4	parcel	The mail carrier brought a **parcel** to the door.	parcel
5	batter	Mother put chocolate chips in the cake **batter**.	batter
6	work	Father goes to **work** early in the morning.	work
7	number	Ten is an even **number**.	number
8	dinner	Mother cooked spaghetti for **dinner**.	dinner
9	lady	Jenna's grandmother is a nice **lady**.	lady
10	hermit	Chris has a **hermit** crab for a pet.	hermit
11	manner	Sydnee has a kind **manner**.	manner
12	use	Please **use** a sharp pencil to write your answers.	use
13	center	The sun is the **center** of our solar system.	center
14	borrow	The neighbor came to **borrow** a cup of sugar.	borrow
15	pinky	The **pinky** finger is the smallest finger on your hand.	pinky
16	lumber	Dan needs more **lumber** for the doghouse.	lumber
17	muffin	Donna had a blueberry **muffin** for breakfast.	muffin
18	pull	The sled dogs will **pull** the sleigh.	pull
19	donkey	Jesus rode on a **donkey** on Palm Sunday.	donkey
20	button	Peter lost a **button** off his coat.	button

LANGUAGE ARTS 209

ALTERNATE LIFEPAC TEST

Name ____________________

Date ____________________

My Score

34 / **42**

Each answer = 1 point

Draw a line from the first part of a compound word to the last part of a compound word.

1.

jelly ▸	◂ sand
fire ▸	◂ crow
quick ▸	◂ place
scare ▸	◂ fish

Write the *be* verbs on the lines.

2. a. ____________________ b. ____________________

c. ____________________ d. ____________________

Read the words. Draw a line (/) between the syllables.

3. a. hornet b. percent

c. candy d. pillow

e. maybe f. banner

g. turtle h. dental

Use the sample dictionary page to answer the questions. Write the answers on the lines.

fig (fĭg), *NOUN*. a small, soft, sweet fruit about the size of a plum. It grows on a tree in warm regions. Figs are usually dried like raisins.

fil·ly (**fĭl** ē), *NOUN*. a young female horse, donkey, or zebra; mare that is less than four or five years old. *PLURAL* fil·lies

fil·thy (**fĭl** thē), *ADJECTIVE*. very dirty; foul: *a filthy shirt*. *ADJECTIVE* filth·i·er, filth·i·est.

finch (fĭnch), *NOUN*. a small songbird with a bill shaped like a cone. *Sparrows, cardinals, and canaries are finches. PLURAL* finch·es.

4. How many words are one syllable? ____________________

5. Write the words that are two syllables.

a. ____________________ b. ____________________

Add a prefix to the underlined word to create a new word.

6. build again ____________

7. not even ____________

8. opposite of cover ____________

9. do again ____________

Read the sentences.
Circle the correct tense of the underlined verb.

10. Ray won his soccer game last Friday.

past **present** **future**

11. Jesus saves us from our sins.

past **present** **future**

12. Neal will climb the tree to get the cat.

past **present** **future**

Write the verb on the line that correctly completes the sentence.

13. Chad and Gabe ____________ in the church choir.
(sing / sings)

14. The monkey ____________ from tree to tree.
(swings / swing)

15. Katelyn ____________ the flute.
(play/ plays)

16. The boys ____________ they can win the softball game.
(hope / hopes)

Write the root word of the words that have a prefix, a suffix, or both.

17. unfriendly ______________________

18. return ______________________

19. untie ______________________

20. jumped ______________________

Put a check mark in the box that has the compound sentence written correctly.

21. a. ☐ Andrea picked the flowers, and, Angie arranged them.

b. ☐ Andrea picked the flowers, and Angie arranged them.

22. a. ☐ Tara likes to sing and Joni likes to play the guitar.

b. ☐ Tara likes to sing, and Joni likes to play the guitar.

23. a. ☐ Bev rode her bike, and Mike ran.

b. ☐ Bev rode her bike and, Mike ran.

Draw a line from the manuscript letter to the cursive letter.

24.

n ▸	◂ *y*
g ▸	◂ *o*
y ▸	◂ *n*
o ▸	◂ *c*
c ▸	◂ *g*

ALTERNATE SPELLING TEST

1	sandy	The beach was warm and **sandy**.	sandy
2	pester	Tim likes to **pester** his younger sister Beth.	pester
3	parrot	Eric's **parrot** knows how to say, "Polly wants a cracker."	parrot
4	off	Please turn **off** the light when you leave the room.	off
5	mister	Using the word **mister** is a polite way to address a man.	mister
6	fellow	A **fellow** can be a man or a boy.	fellow
7	rusty	The old car was very **rusty**.	rusty
8	person	Who is that **person** standing over there?	person
9	yellow	**Yellow** is Sara's favorite color.	yellow
10	many	There are **many** people in New York City.	many
11	napkin	Please use a **napkin** to wipe your mouth after eating spaghetti.	napkin
12	rugged	The Rocky Mountains are large and **rugged**.	rugged
13	ruby	Sally has a beautiful **ruby** necklace.	ruby
14	wonder	I **wonder** what heaven will be like.	wonder
15	narrow	The truck driver carefully drove over the **narrow** bridge.	narrow
16	very	Kaden was **very** excited to see his grandma.	very
17	sister	Nick likes to take care of his younger **sister**.	sister
18	dinner	Anna wants to know what's for **dinner**.	dinner
19	use	This cookie recipe says to **use** three eggs.	use
20	kitten	Darren's **kitten** has soft, white fur.	kitten

LANGUAGE ARTS 210

Unit 10: Looking Back

TEACHER NOTES

MATERIALS NEEDED FOR LIFEPAC	
Required	Suggested
• sharp pencil	• crayons or colored pencils • notebook or composition book for journaling • paper with guidelines for Spelling Tests

ADDITIONAL LEARNING ACTIVITIES

Sections 1-3

Select any activities from the previous units that were either not done or that need additional review for this unit.

Suggested Books:

Read or review any of the books from previous lists.

Journal Suggestions:

1. Have the students write in their journals about their favorite poem(s) or story covered this year.
2. Have the student write about the meaning of one of the following sayings and phrases.

   Back to the drawing board
   Better late than never
   Cold feet
   Don't cry over spilled milk.
   Don't judge a book by its cover.
   Easier said than done
   Eaten out of house and home
   Get a taste of your own medicine
   Got up on the wrong side of the bed
   In hot water
   Keep your fingers crossed.
   Practice what you preach.
   Two heads are better than one.
   Turn over a new leaf
   Where there's a will, there's a way.
   You can't teach an old dog new tricks.

3. Have each student write about which topics they think will be included in Grade 3 Language Arts.

Suggested Books:

(This is the list of suggested poems from *Core Knowledge Sequence: Content Guidelines for Grades K-8)*

Bad in Summer by Robert Louis Stevenson
Caterpillars by Aileen Fisher
Discovery by Harry Behn
Harriet Tubman by Eloise Greenfield
Hurt No Living Thing by Christina Rossetti
Lincoln by Nancy Byrd Turner
Rudolph is Tired of the City by Gwendolyn Brooks
Smart by Shel Silverstein
Something Told the Wild Geese by Rachel Field
There Was an Old Man with a Beard by Edward Lear
Who Has Seen the Wind by Christina Georgina Rossetti (in student's Unit 6)
Windy Nights by Robert Louis Stevenson

Administer the LIFEPAC Spelling Test.
The test is provided in this Teacher's Guide.
Evaluate the tests and review the words the students spelled incorrectly.
If necessary, review all of the words in the unit to prepare for the alternate spelling test.
Administer the Alternate LIFEPAC Spelling test that is provided in this Teacher's Guide.

Administer the LIFEPAC Test.
The test is to be administered in one session. Give no help except with directions.
Evaluate the tests and review areas where the students have done poorly.
Review the pages and activities that stress the concepts tested.
If necessary, administer the Alternate LIFEPAC Test.

ANSWER KEYS

SECTION 1

1.1
1. *place, grace*
2. delay, away
3. city, pity
4. away, day
5. board, Lord
6. everything, thinking
7. fro, go
8. cry, die
9. deep, sleep
10. sinned, wind
11. fault, out
12. ill, will
13. sea, be
14. down, drown
15. soul, whole
16. wish, fish
17. queasy, easy
18. around, ground
19. about, out
20. land, sand
21. disobeyed, stayed
22. sea, agree
23. glory, story
24. wrong, strong

1.2 *dill*, fill, gill, hill, kill, mill, pill, quill, till, sill, will

1.3 *den*, hen, Ken, men, pen, ten, when

1.4 *dam*, ham, jam, ram, yam

1.5 *ban*, can, fan, man, pan, ran, tan, van

1.6 *bay*, day, hay, Kay, lay, may, pay, ray, say, way

1.7 *date*, fate, gate, hate, late, mate, rate

1.8
a. mile b. song
c. pail d. toy
e. fat f. west

1.9 Possible answers:
a. made
b. these
c. been, here
d. here, been
e. before
f. because
g. sometimes
h. house
i. white
j. gave
k. money
l. one

1.10 Any order within categories:

CVC	**CVCV**	**CVVC**
get	bone	seat
lip	hope	coat
can	tale	beet
box	kite	tail
web	cube	leap
bag	fine	nail
mob	save	foam

1.11 b**a**g p**i**g b**u**s b**e**d b**o**x

1.12 rake leaf kite boat

1.13 **h**en **f**ish **w**olf **g**oat **t**urtle

1.14 g z m r p

1.15
a. eehps sheep
b. auwrsl walrus
c. kwah hawk
d. aels seal
e. noli lion

1.16
a. toad b. meet c. doe
d. mean e. glue f. lie
g. jeep h. team i. true
j. jail k. tie l. boat

1.17
a. tr**ee** b. l**ea**f
c. p**ie** d. s**oa**p
e. g**oa**t f. bl**ue**
g. p**ai**l

1.18

day	guy
monkey	pause
buy	donkey
cause	ray
jaw	flew
dew	law

1.19
a. sound
b. toy
c. boil
d. ouch
e. cow
f. joy
g. coin
h. crowd
i. noun
j. down
k. join
l. boy

1.20 Any order within categories:
a. good, hook, cook, look, wood
b. boo, bloom, food, zoo, fool

1.21 sometimes

1.22 Any order:
because, made, before, one, gave
here, these, house, white

1.23 been, money

1.24 Any order within categories:
a. chef, pie, soup, bread, cookie, recipe, salad, oven, carrots, blender
b. bake, follow, pour, fry, read, cooked, eat, mixing, stir, chew, create

1.25 Any order: are, is, was, were

1.26
a. noun
b. verb
c. noun
d. verb
e. noun
f. verb
g. verb
h. noun

1.27
a. P b. C
c. C d. P
e. P f. C
g. C h. P
i. C j. P
k. C l. P
m. P n. C
o. C p. P
q. P r. C
s. P t. C
u. C v. P
w. P x. C

1.28 b. Proper nouns begin with a capital letter.

1.29 Suggested answers:
a. city b. lake
c. state d. store
e. girl, sister f. pop, soda, drink

1.30 Student answers – Teacher check

1.31
a. before
b. house
c. because
d. made
e. one
f. Sometimes
g. these
h. money
i. gave
j. white
k. here
l. been

1.32
1. God told Jonah to go to Nineveh.
2. Jonah went to Tarshish instead.
3. God sent a windy storm on the sea.
4. The men threw Jonah in the water.
5. A large fish swallowed Jonah.
6. The fish spat Jonah out on dry land.
7. Jonah finally went to Nineveh.

1.33 Teacher check

1.34 Teacher check

1.35 See below:

j	x	z	j	b	r	a	v	e	x	z	j
x	z	j	x	z	j	q	u	i	e	t	x
j	x	c	l	o	w	n	j	x	z	j	x
z	j	x	z	j	f	r	o	s	t	x	z
x	s	l	i	m	z	j	x	z	j	x	z
j	x	z	j	x	z	j	c	r	e	a	m
s	h	a	r	e	x	z	j	x	z	j	x
z	j	x	t	h	u	m	p	z	j	x	z
b	l	o	c	k	j	x	z	j	x	z	j
z	x	j	x	z	j	x	z	w	h	y	j
x	z	j	x	z	j	d	r	o	p	x	z
j	f	l	a	g	x	z	j	x	z	j	x
z	j	x	z	j	p	r	a	y	x	z	j
x	z	j	x	z	j	g	l	o	b	e	x
z	j	x	z	j	x	z	c	h	u	r	n
j	x	g	r	a	d	e	z	j	x	z	j
x	p	l	e	a	s	e	z	j	x	z	j
z	x	j	x	z	j	x	t	r	e	e	z

	a. block	b. clown
	c. flag	d. globe
	e. please	f. slim
	g. churn	h. share
	i. thump	j. why
	k. brave	l. cream
	m. drop	n. frost
	o. grade	p. pray
	q. tree	r. quiet
1.36	a. gift	b. cold
	c. limp	d. grind
	e. sing	f. bank
	g. slant	h. ask
	i. last	j. wink
	k. mind	l. lamp
	m. rest	n. desk
	o. bunt	p. ring
	q. raft	r. bold
	s. band	t. wimp

1.37	a. laugh	b. phone	c. cough
	d. elephant	e. phonics	f. rough
1.38	a. knit	b. sign	c. calf
	d. lamb	e. yolk	f. rhubarb
	g. write	h. light	i. moss
	j. salmon	k. gnome	l. knife

1.39	rain / bow	pil / low
	pan / cake	rib / bon
	sail / boat	bar / rel
	pop / corn	muf / fin
	shoe / lace	sum / mer
	can / dle	win / dow
	thim / ble	lum / ber
	jun / gle	wal / rus
	waf / fle	pic / nic
	whis / tle	win / ter

1.40 Any order:
rainbow, pancake, sailboat, popcorn, shoelace

1.41 Any order:
candle, thimble, jungle, waffle, whistle

1.42 Any order:
window, lumber, walrus, picnic, winter

1.43 Teacher check

SELF TEST 1

1.01 Jonah was a prophet of God.
1.02 God told Jonah to go to Nineveh.
1.03 A large fish swallowed Jonah.
1.04 wish
fish
1.05 desk
1.06 talk
1.07 are, is, was, were
1.08 city, man, dog
1.09 Joshua, Denver, Fido

1.010	a. boat	b. sheep	c. team
	d. clue	e. pause	f. monkey

1.011 good food zoo look bloom wood
1.012 knife
1.013 gnat
1.014 a. car / pet
b. min / now
c. jun / gle
1.015 head
1.016 headlight

SECTION 2

2.1
- ☒ God told Jonah to go to Nineveh.
- ☐ Got on a ship.
- ☒ The ship went to Tarshish.
- ☐ God.
- ☒ The men were scared.
- ☒ Jonah slept.
- ☐ Water.
- ☐ The men.
- ☒ A large fish swallowed Jonah.
- ☐ Was smelly and yucky.
- ☐ Made the fish spit out Jonah on dry land.

2.2
a. **Jonah** got on a ship **.**
b. God **sent a strong wind .**
c. Water **splashed in the ship .** *or* **!**
d. The men **threw Jonah in the water .** *or* **!**
e. **The belly of the fish** was smelly and yucky **.** *or* **!**
f. **God** made the fish spit out Jonah on dry land **.**

2.3

declarative sentence	?
interrogative sentence	!
exclamatory sentence	.

2.4
a. . b. ?
c. . d. ! (*or* .)
e. . f. . (*or* !)
g. ? h. !
i. ? j. .

2.5 Possible answers:
a. right, night
b. many, very
c. would
d. found
e. knew
f. your
g. always
h. should
i. through
j. around
k. night, right
l. very, many

2.6
Alex Andrews
222 Main Street
Mesa, AZ 45689

Jon Jacobs
123 N. Idaho Ave.
Pine Tree, AZ 45678

2.7

Alaska	ME
Kansas	OR
Maine	WI
Maryland	AK
Oregon	KS
Wisconsin	MD

2.8 See below:

n	i	g	h	t	f	o	m	a	n	y	v
y	o	o	u	w	o	u	l	d	i	u	e
o	t	h	r	o	u	g	h	z	g	x	r
r	y	o	u	r	n	r	i	g	h	t	y
s	h	o	u	l	d	a	r	o	u	n	d
b	k	n	e	w	p	a	l	w	a	y	s

2.9 See below:

eat	pure	forget	power	make	plug	box
recycle	seed	unkind	dish	rewrite	help	untie
unplug	play	remake	fill	undo	count	refill
good	talk	quick	walk	jump	sad	tie
helpful	play	freshness	kind	countless	thank	fairly
seedless	sick	toys	fair	sadly	write	cheerful
jumping	plate	girls	fresh	walking	bike	forgetful
quickly	girl	boxes	do	talked	toy	powerless
goodness	law	dishes	cup	played	love	purely
sickness	quiet	playful	need	thankful	sorrow	eating

2.10 4

2.11 Any order:
pure, plate, write, bike, love, tie, need, make, seed

2.12

seedless	not happy
kindly	full of cheer
rewrite	no seeds
cheerful	good action
goodness	in a kind way
unhappy	write again

2.13
a. dogs b. puppies
c. mice d. sheep
e. horses f. monkeys
g. turtles h. walruses
i. foxes j. deer
k. finches l. bunnies

2.14 always, around, found, knew, many, night, right, should, through, very, would, your

2.15
a. Jimmy had a peanut butter and jelly sandwich for lunch.
b. Allison goes to bed at 8:00.
c. Greg will take out the garbage.
d. David is crying because he fell with his bike.
e. Kelly is going to her piano lesson this afternoon.
f. Anna lives in a yellow house on Pine Street.

2.16 Teacher check – answers will vary

2.17
(a.) Michael's dog ran away.
(b.) The dog's leash was broken.
c. Michael and his sisters looked for the dog.
(d.) They found the dog in their neighbor's yard.
e. Michael and his sisters were happy they found the dog.

2.18
a. isn't b they're
c. I'm d won't
e. he'll f. shouldn't
g. she's h couldn't
i. it's j. we're

2.19
a. Tomorrow **we'll** be going to the zoo.
b. **I'm** excited about tomorrow!
c. **We're** hoping to see an elephant.
d. An elephant **isn't** a small animal.
e. **It's** the largest of all land animals.
f. An elephant **can't** be a house pet!

2.20 Teacher check
2.21 Teacher check
2.22 Teacher check
2.23 Teacher check
2.24 Teacher check
2.25 Teacher check

2.26

e	*t*	r	*d*
l	*e*	d	*o*
t	*m*	i	*r*
m	*l*	o	*i*

2.27 Teacher check
2.28 Teacher check
2.29 Teacher check

2.30
a. run b. easy
c. many d. fast
e. lost f. low
g. short h. old
i. poor j. weak
k. tall l. dry

2.31 See below:

e	a	s	y	w	e	a	k
p	d	z	x	f	a	s	t
o	r	q	r	t	a	l	l
o	y	w	u	l	o	w	o
r	m	a	n	y	k	p	s
o	l	d	s	h	o	r	t

2.32
h
f
a
i
b
g
j
d
e
c

2.33
a. Main b. by, flower
c. buy, for d. blew
e. blue f. son, flower
g. new h. knew, would, be

SELF TEST 2

2.01 Any order:
fast – slow
hot – cold
old – new
on – off
2.02 Any order:
quiet – silent
happy – glad
sick – ill
tiny – small
2.03 Any order:
dear – deer
plane – plain
right – write
weak – week
2.04 unkind
2.05 remake
2.06 refill
2.07 kindness
2.08 making
2.09 filling
2.010 nouns
2.011 ladies
2.012 boxes
2.013 wishes
2.014 b
2.015 a
2.016 mother's
2.017 they're
2.018 he'll
2.019 isn't
2.020 I'm
2.021 she's
2.022 a. heading
b. greeting
c. body
d. closing
e. signature

SECTION 3

3.1 Possible answers:
a. didn't
b. don't
c. first
d. its
e. off
f. soon
g. tell
h. their
i. then
j. work, went
k. went, work
l. which
3.2 a. will go
b. will swim
c. will make
d. will eat
e. will be
3.3 a. want
b. ask
c. walk
d. follows
e. look
3.4 a. wanted
b. asked
c. walked
d. followed
e. looked
f. ed
3.5 a. helped b. help
c. will help d. fixed
e. fix f. will fix
g. crawled h. crawls
i. will crawl
3.6 a. past
b. future
c. present
d. present
e. past
f. future
g. present
3.7 a. The duck floats on the water.
b. Kelly and Jan giggle at the clown.
c. Fluffy is a cat.
d. The turtle and the snail were slow.
3.8 a. jumps
b. play
c. bounces
d. flies
e. run
f. wins

3.9 a. didn't = did + not
b. don't = do + not

3.10 tell, off

3.11 soon

3.12 Teacher check

3.13 a. Carter
b. Star Street
c. Tony
d. Patty's Pet Place
e. Carter
f. (555) 345-6785
g. Moon Street

3.14

a. didn't	b. don't
c. first	d. its
e. off	f. soon
g. tell	h. their
i. then	j. work
k. went	l. which

3.15 a. plaid
b. pipeline
c. pivot
d. pious, piping, plaid
e. 13
f. pistil
g. pita, pizza
h. in alphabetical order

3.16

ape	lizard
bear	monkey
buffalo	mule
camel	parrot
crow	rabbit
deer	sheep
elephant	turtle
goat	weasel
horse	wolf
iguana	zebra
koala	

3.17 Teacher check

3.18 a. My friend **J**anet lives in **H**awaii.
b. **T**he state of Hawaii is made up of many islands**.**
c. It is in the **P**acific **O**cean.
d. **I**t is **a** beautiful state.
e. **J**anet asked if **I** would like to visit her in Hawaii.

3.19 a. He
b. They
c. her
d. them
e. She
f. it

3.20 a. Lisa had a birthday party.
b. Mother made a pretty cake.
c. The cake had white frosting.
d. It had pretty flowers.
e. That cake had candles!
f. I saw eight candles on the cake.

3.21 Teacher check

3.22 a. Mother cleaned the fridge, and Father took out the trash.
b. Nathan swept the floor, and Nick washed the dishes.
c. The kitchen was clean, and Mother was happy.
d. Guests were coming for dinner, and the house was clean.

3.23 Teacher check

3.24 Teacher check

3.25 Teacher check

3.26

a. alwais	always
b. thier	their
c. becawse	because
d. theze	these
e. befour	before
f. verry	very
g. do'nt	don't
h. wich	which
i. rihte	right
j. gaiv	gave
k. sumtimes	sometimes
l. yore	your

SELF TEST 3

3.01 past
3.02 future
3.03 present
3.04 Lacy walks her dog to the park.
3.05 Justin and Lance play tennis together.
3.06 Fluffy is a white cat.
3.07 Clay Street
3.08 Harold's Hardware
3.09 Flora's Flowers
3.010 a. **L**ee rode his bike to **J**ack's house.
b. Jack'**s** house is on **O**ak Street.
c. **T**he boys rode their bikes to the park**.**
3.011 a. her
b. he
c. She
3.012 a. many
b. green
c. baby
3.013
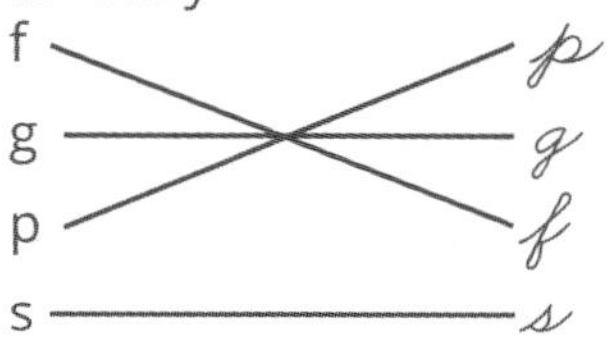

UNIT REVIEW

1. .
2. ?
3. .
4. !, . (*or* !)
5. many, beautiful
6. Joe and Jane went to the beach.
7. They made a sand castle.
8. They used a bucket and shovel.
9. Joe put a flag on top.
10. Mother took a picture of them.
11. a. action, whisper
wiggle, subtract, giggle, clapping,
running, holler
b. was, are, were, is
12. be verbs
13. whis / per
wig / gle
hol / ler
14. a. renew, unhappy, recycle, rewrite, unplug
b. helpless, talked, quickly, hopeful, boxes
15.
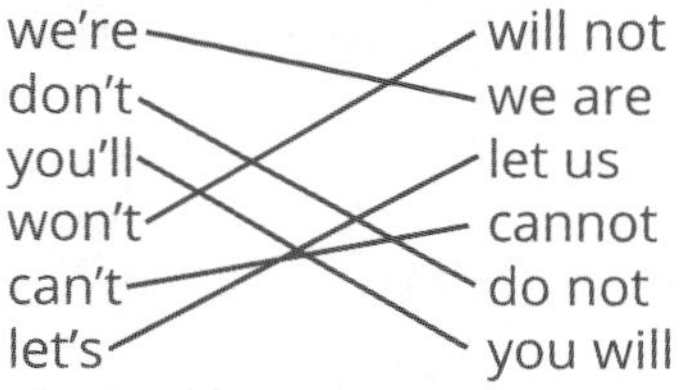
16. ✓ God loves me.
Gave us the Bible.
Stories about how God took care of His people.
✓ We can learn about God from the Bible.
✓ It is good to read the Bible.
17. boats, wishes, boxes, geese, sheep, deer, toys, ladies
18. a. Baby dogs are called puppies.
b. Baby cats are called kittens.
c. Red, orange, yellow, green, blue, indigo, and violet are the colors of the rainbow.
19. fish
20. Teacher check

LIFEPAC TEST

1. river, father, rat
2. Maine, Denver, Pam
3. noun
4. verb
5. Suggested answer:
   Kelly went hiking in the desert.
6. Suggested answer:
   She took two bottles of water with her.
7. subject
8. verb
9. June, Sarah, Dallas
10. I, Christmas
11. .
    !
    ?
12. cats
13. dishes
14. toys
15. babies
16. feet
17. moose
18. brown
19. two
20. bad
21. b
22. a
23. b
24. helpful
25. replace
26. popcorn
27. a. past
    b. present
    c. future
28. a. wig / gle b. pic / nic
    c. ban / ner d. sail / boat

ALTERNATE LIFEPAC TEST

1. sister
2. Mary
3. noun
4. verb
5. The dog chased the cat.
6. A newspaper is black and white and read all over.
7. Dogs bark.
8. july, i
9. declarative sentence — .
   exclamatory sentence — !
   interrogative sentence — ?
10. cows
11. patches
12. boys
13. ladies
14. mice
15. sheep
16. purple
17. three
18. b
19. a
20. b
21. wanting
22. unhappy
23. doghouse
24. present
25. past
26. future
27. a. gig /gle b. mas / ter
    c. win / ner d. fire / fly

SPELLING TEST

1	gave	My mom **gave** me some grapes for a snack.	gave
2	its	The dog is chasing **its** tail.	its
3	tell	I want to **tell** you a secret.	tell
4	off	Please turn **off** the light when you leave the room.	off
5	these	**These** are your toys.	these
6	went	She **went** for a long walk.	went
7	made	Grandmother **made** the birthday cake.	made
8	always	It is **always** morning somewhere in the world.	always
9	money	She received **money** for her birthday.	money
10	soon	I hope I get a puppy **soon**!	soon
11	because	She was dirty **because** she fell in a mud puddle.	because
12	before	The letter *a* comes **before** the letter *b* in the alphabet.	before
13	first	She was **first** in line to go down the slide.	first
14	their	The family loves **their** dog.	their
15	then	The cat drank the milk **then** licked its paws.	then
16	which	Jason had to decide **which** present to open first.	which
17	white	The **white** snow glittered brightly.	white
18	around	The runners ran **around** the track.	around
19	found	The girl **found** her cat in the garage.	found
20	house	They painted their **house** a bright green.	house

LANGUAGE ARTS 210

ALTERNATE LIFEPAC TEST

Name ____________________

Date ____________________

Each answer = 1 point

Complete this activity.

1.	Circle the common noun.	Mary	sister
2.	Circle the proper noun.	Mary	sister

Read the sentences.
Identify the underlined word and circle the correct answer.

3.	<u>Sydnee</u> has a new baby brother	noun	verb
4.	She <u>likes</u> to hold him.	noun	verb

Circle the group of words that is a complete sentence.

5. The dog chased the cat.

Chased the cat.

Read the question. Circle the answer that is a complete sentence.

6. What is black and white and read all over?

A newspaper.

A newspaper is black and white and read all over.

Read the sentence. Underline the noun and circle the verb.

7. Dogs bark.

Read the words. Circle the words that should be capitalized.

8. july grass flower nightweed i

Draw a line from the type of sentence to the correct punctuation mark.

9.

declarative sentence ▸	◂ ?
exclamatory sentence ▸	◂ .
interrogative sentence ▸	◂ !

Choose the correct way to write a plural noun.
Write the word on the line.

10.	cow	____________	cows	cowes
11.	patch	____________	patches	patchs
12.	boy	____________	boies	boys
13.	lady	____________	ladys	ladies
14.	mouse	____________	mouses	mice
15.	sheep	____________	sheep	sheeps

Read the sentences. Circle the adjective that describes the underlined noun in each sentence.

16. Nancy wore a purple <u>coat</u>.

17. Jill saw three <u>eagles</u>.

Read the sentences. Put an X next to the sentence that has the possessive noun written correctly.

18. a. ☐ Emmas' pencil broke.
b. ☐ Emma's pencil broke.

19. a. ☐ John's bicycle has a flat tire.
b. ☐ Johns' bicycle has a flat tire.

20. a. ☐ The farmers' barn is clean.
b. ☐ The farmer's barn is clean.

Read the words. Circle the word that has a suffix.

21. unhappy wanting doghouse

Read the words. Underline the word that has a prefix.

22. unhappy wanting doghouse

Read the words. Draw a box around the compound word.

23. unhappy wanting doghouse

Read the sentences. Circle the correct tense of the underlined verb.

24.	Olivia <u>talks</u> on the phone.	**past**	**present**	**future**
25.	Yesterday Olivia <u>talked</u> to Grandmother.	**past**	**present**	**future**
26.	Olivia <u>will talk</u> to Uncle Steve tomorrow.	**past**	**present**	**future**

Draw a line (/) between the two syllables of the words.

27. a. g i g g l e b. m a s t e r

c. w i n n e r d. f i r e f l y

ALTERNATE SPELLING TEST			
1	should	You **should** not run with scissors.	should
2	through	He ran **through** the house with dirty shoes.	through
3	would	She **would** love to have a birthday party.	would
4	your	It is important to brush **your** teeth.	your
5	been	He hasn't **been** to the dentist for a long time.	been
6	didn't	I **didn't** do it.	didn't
7	don't	**Don't** you want some chocolate chip cookies?	don't
8	night	An owl likes to hunt at **night.**	night
9	right	He gave the **right** answer to the problem.	right
10	sometimes	**Sometimes** we play games after supper.	sometimes
11	here	You are **here** taking a spelling test.	here
12	knew	He **knew** how to write in cursive.	knew
13	one	The softball team only scored **one** point.	one
14	many	There are **many** people in New York City.	many
15	very	Kaden was **very** excited to see his grandma.	very
16	work	Father goes to **work** early in the morning.	work
17	tell	It is important to always **tell** the truth.	tell
18	off	Remember to turn **off** the light when you leave the room.	off
19	went	The family **went** on vacation to the Grand Canyon.	went
20	because	Jesus died for us **because** He loves us!	because

TEACHER RESOURCES

SECOND GRADE SPELLING LISTS

1-1 (Short Vowels)

bad
fast
best
tell
went
yet
its
sit
trip
wish
hot
us

1-2 (Long Vowel Sounds with Silent e)

gave
made
name
sale
these
five
line
nice
ride
write
joke
tune

1-3 (Vowel Digraphs)

pail
rain
green
mean
meek
need
read
sleep
coat
float
goes
suit

2-1 (Vowel Digraphs ay, ey, ue, uy)

always
hay
played
key
money
monkey
blue
clue
due
true
buy
guy

2-2 (Vowel Digraphs au, aw, eu)

because
fraud
haul
pause
fawn
hawk
jaw
law
chew
dew
flew
stew

2-3 (Sounds of oo)

food
cool
moon
pool
soon
zoo
cook
hood
hook
shook
took
wood

3-1 (r-Controlled Vowels)

farm
park
fern
term
first
girl
before
hurt
more
or
sport
burn

3-2 (Beginning Consonant Blends)

broom
crate
drum
fry
gray
prize
trail
blade
close
plate
flat
glad

3-3 (Ending Consonant Blends)

left
gift
hold
ramp
lump
land
wind
junk
ant
desk
list
most

SECOND GRADE SPELLING LISTS

4-1 (Consonant Digraphs sh, ch, wh)

chain
chat
chess
quit
shame
sheep
their
thin
third
those
whale
wheel

4-2 (Beginning Consonant Digraphs)

children
chip
quail
quiet
share
shark
short
then
this
while
white
why

4-3 (Ending Consonant Digraphs)

rich
which
neck
rock
sack
dish
fish
rush
wash
both
math
path

5-1 (Diphthongs ou, ow)

around
count
found
house
loud
noun
crowd
crown
fowl
owl
town
wow

5-2 (Diphthongs oi, oy)

boy
employ
joy
loyal
oyster
toy
boil
coin
joint
moist
point
soil

5-3 (Rule Breakers)

enough
dough
should
thought
through
would
your
blow
crow
slow
sow
toward

6-1 (Contractions)

can't
didn't
don't
hasn't
won't
it's
he's
that's
they're
we're
I'm
I've

Curtain
Picture

6-2 (Word Families – Rhyming Words)

been
den
right
night
cold
gold
ship
whip
call
hall
plank
sank

holiday
January

6-3 (Compound Words)

upon
outside
sometimes
mailbox
raincoat
pigpen
baseball
birthday
without
notebook
beehive
waterfall

SECOND GRADE SPELLING LISTS

7-1 (Soft c and g, z Sound of s)
- cent
- city
- lace
- slice
- age
- cage
- gem
- gym
- cause
- please
- raise
- does

7-2 (Silent Consonants)
- sign
- sigh
- high
- light
- might
- lamb
- comb
- knew
- knife
- wrap
- mess
- loss

7-3 (Homonyms)
- know
- no
- tail
- tale
- dear
- deer
- here
- hear
- weak
- week
- one
- won

8-1 (More Beginning Consonant Blends)
- skate
- snap
- scold
- small
- spoon
- step
- swim
- twin
- scrape
- split
- spray
- stray

8-2 (Ending Consonant Blends ng and dge)
- bang
- fang
- sung
- thing
- long
- sing
- edge
- ledge
- badge
- ridge
- lodge
- fudge

8-3 (Beginning and Ending Consonant Blends)
- snack
- church
- skunk
- stand
- thick
- grind
- crash
- stink
- truck
- truth
- bleach
- clock

9-1 (Words that End in y)
- lady
- rainy
- pinky
- sandy
- rusty
- ruby
- very
- many
- off
- pull
- use
- work

9-2 (Syllabication Rules)
- kitten
- dinner
- borrow
- button
- fellow
- rugged
- narrow
- yellow
- parrot
- muffin
- manner
- batter

9-3 (Syllabication Rules)
- sister
- number
- center
- donkey
- mister
- napkin
- wonder
- person
- pester
- lumber
- hermit
- parcel

10-1 (Review)
- because
- been
- before
- gave
- here
- house
- made
- money
- one
- sometimes
- these
- white

10-2 (Review)
- always
- around
- found
- knew
- many
- night
- right
- should
- through
- very
- would
- your

10-3 (Review)
- didn't
- don't
- first
- its
- off
- tell
- their
- then
- soon
- went
- which
- work

ALPHABETIZED SECOND GRADE SPELLING LISTS

age (7-1)
always (2-1)
ant (3-3)
around (5-1)
bad (1-1)
badge (2-1)
bang (2-1)
baseball (6-3)
batter (9-2)
because (2-2)
beehive (6-3)
been (6-2)
before (3-1)
best (1-1)
birthday (6-3)
blade (3-2)
bleach (8-3)
blow (5-3)
blue (2-1)
boil (5-2)
borrow (9-2)
both (4-3)
boy (5-2)
broom (3-2)
burn (3-1)
button (9-2)
buy (2-1)
cage (7-1)
call (6-2)
can't (6-1)
cause (7-1)
cent (7-1)
center (9-3)
chain (4-1)
chat (4-1)
chess (4-1)
chew (2-2)
children (4-2)
chip (4-2)
church (8-3)
city (7-1)
clock (8-3)
close (3-2)
clue (2-1)
coat (1-3)
coin (5-2)
cold (6-2)
comb (7-2)
cook (2-3)
cool (2-3)
count (5-1)
crash (8-3)
crate (3-2)
crow (5-3)
crowd (5-1)
crown (5-1)
dear (7-3)
deer (7-3)
den (6-2)
desk (3-3)
dew (2-2)
didn't (6-1)
dinner (9-2)
dish (4-3)
does (7-1)
donkey (9-3)
don't (6-1)
dough (5-3)
drum (3-2)
due (2-1)
edge (8-2)
employ (5-2)
enough (5-3)
fang (8-2)
farm (3-1)
fast (1-1)
fawn (2-2)
fellow (9-2)
fern (3-1)
first (3-1)
fish (4-3)
five (1-2)
flat (3-2)
flew (2-2)
float (1-3)
food (2-3)
found (5-1)
fowl (5-1)
fraud (2-2)
fry (3-2)
fudge (8-2)
gave (1-2)
gem (7-1)
gift (3-3)
girl (3-1)
glad (3-2)
goes (1-3)
gold (6-2)
gray (3-2)
green (1-3)
grind (8-3)
guy (2-1)
gym (7-1)
hall (6-2)
hasn't (6-1)
haul (2-2)
hawk (2-2)
hay (2-1)
hear (7-3)
here (7-3)
hermit (9-3)
he's (6-1)
high (7-2)
hold (3-3)
hood (2-3)
hook (2-3)
hot (1-1)
house (5-1)
hurt (3-1)
its (1-1)
it's (6-1)
I'm (6-1)
I've (6-1)
jaw (2-2)
joint (5-2)
joke (1-2)
joy (5-2)
junk (3-3)
key (2-1)
kitten (9-2)
knew (7-2)
knife (7-2)
know (7-3)
lace (7-1)
lady (9-1)
lamb (7-2)
land (3-3)
law (2-2)
ledge (8-2)
left (3-3)
light (7-2)
line (1-2)
list (3-3)
lodge (8-2)
long (8-2)
loss (7-2)
loud (5-1)
loyal (5-2)
lumber (9-3)
lump (3-3)
made (1-2)
mailbox (6-3)
manner (9-2)
many (9-1)
math (4-3)
mean (1-3)
meek (1-3)
mess (7-2)
might (7-2)

mister (9-3)
moist (5-2)
money (2-1)
monkey (2-1)
moon (2-3)
more (3-1)
most (3-3)
muffin (9-2)
name (1-2)
napkin (9-3)
narrow (9-2)
neck (4-3)
need (1-3)
nice (1-2)
night (6-2)
no (7-3)
notebook (6-3)
noun (5-1)
number (9-3)
off (9-1)
one (7-3)
or (3-1)
outside (6-3)
owl (5-1)
oyster (5-2)
pail (1-3)
parcel (9-3)
park (3-1)
parrot (9-2)
path (4-3)
pause (2-2)
person (9-3)
pester (9-3)
pigpen (6-3)
pinky (9-1)
plank (6-2)
plate (3-2)
played (2-1)
please (7-1)
point (5-2)
pool (2-3)
prize (3-2)
pull (9-1)
quail (4-2)
quiet (4-2)
quit (4-1)
rain (1-3)
raincoat (6-3)
rainy (9-1)
raise (7-1)
ramp (3-3)
read (1-3)
rich (4-3)
ride (1-2)
ridge (8-2)
right (6-2)
rock (4-3)
rug (9-1)
rugged (9-2)
rush (4-3)
rusty (9-1)
sack (4-3)
sale (1-2)
sandy (9-1)
sank (6-2)
scold (8-1)
scrape (8-1)
shame (4-1)
share (4-2)
shark (4-2)
sheep (4-1)
ship (6-2)
shook (2-3)
short (4-2)
should (5-3)
sigh (7-2)
sign (7-2)
sing (8-2)
sister (9-3)
sit (1-1)
skate (8-1)
skunk (8-3)
sleep (1-3)
slice (7-1)
slow (5-3)
small (8-1)
snack (8-3)
snap (8-1)
soil (5-2)
sometimes (6-3)
soon (2-3)
sow (5-3)
split (8-1)
spoon (8-1)
sport (3-1)
spray (8-1)
stand (8-3)
step (8-1)
stew (2-2)
stink (8-3)
stray (8-1)
suit (1-3)
sung (8-2)
swim (8-1)
tail (7-3)
tale (7-3)
tell (1-1)
term (3-1)
that's (6-1)
their (4-1)
then (4-2)
these (1-2)
they're (6-1)
thick (8-3)
thin (4-1)
thing (8-2)
third (4-1)
this (4-2)
those (4-1)
thought (5-3)
through (5-3)
took (2-3)
toward (5-3)
town (5-1)
toy (5-2)
trail (3-2)
trip (1-1)
truck (8-3)
true (2-1)
truth (8-3)
tune (1-2)
twin (8-1)
upon (6-3)
us (1-1)
use (9-1)
very (9-1)
wash (4-3)
waterfall (6-3)
weak (7-3)
week (7-3)
went (1-1)
we're (6-1)
whale (4-1)
wheel (4-1)
which (4-3)
while (4-2)
whip (6-2)
white (4-2)
why (4-2)
wind (3-3)
wish (1-1)
without (6-3)
won (7-3)
wonder (9-3)
won't (6-1)
wood (2-3)
work (9-1)
would (5-3)
wow (5-1)
wrap (7-2)
write (1-2)
yellow (9-2)
yet (1-1)
your (5-3)
zoo (2-3)

LANGUAGE ARTS MANIPULATIVES: WORD FAMILIES

Note:

These Word Families manipulatives may be reproduced on cardstock and cut out. Students can use these manipulatives for word blending practice or other activities the teacher may choose. Discuss with students which words are real and which words are not. Have students create as many "real" words as possible by sliding the strips through the slits on each of the cards.

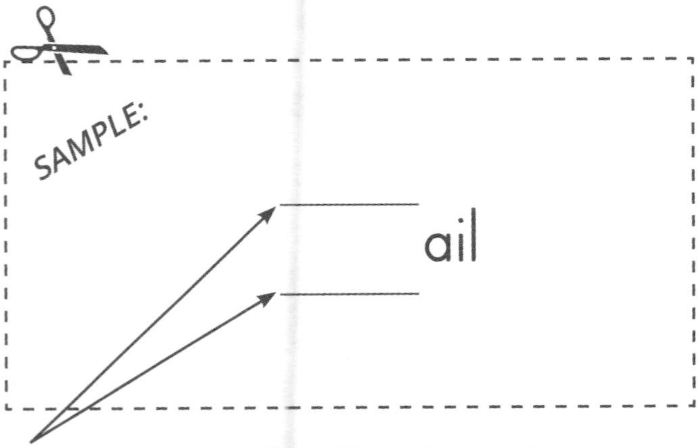

Use an X-Acto™ knife or sharp scissors to cut along the lines to create slits for the strips to slide through.

b
c
d
f
g
h
j
k
l
m
n
p
qu
r
s
t
v
w
x
y
z

ch
sh
th
wh
sp
sl
sc
sm
st
sk
sn
sw
tw
br
tr
gr
fr
dr
cr
pr

wr
bl
cl
fl
gl
pl
str
scr
squ
spl
thr

___at	___all
___ap	___ate
___an	___are
___en	___ub

___ail	___ain
___ay	___ake
___aw	___eat
___ave	___ear

____ide

____ike

____ine

____ow

____eep

____old

____ice

____oop

___oke	___ank
___ook	___ell
___ore	___ash
___ack	___ent

___est	___ip
___in	___ill
___ick	___ot
___ing	___op

___ush	___um
___ock	___ug
___ump	___un
___ed	___im

_____amp

_____oat

_____ump

_____ope

_____ew

_____ist

Spelling Unit/Section ____________ **Name** ______________________________

1. ______________________________ 13. ______________________________
2. ______________________________ 14. ______________________________
3. ______________________________ 15. ______________________________
4. ______________________________ 16. ______________________________
5. ______________________________ 17. ______________________________
6. ______________________________ 18. ______________________________
7. ______________________________ 19. ______________________________
8. ______________________________ 20. ______________________________
9. ______________________________ 21. ______________________________
10. ______________________________ 22. ______________________________
11. ______________________________ 23. ______________________________
12. ______________________________ 24. ______________________________

Spelling Unit/Section ____________ **Name** ______________________________

1. ______________________
2. ______________________
3. ______________________
4. ______________________
5. ______________________
6. ______________________
7. ______________________
8. ______________________
9. ______________________
10. ______________________
11. ______________________
12. ______________________
13. ______________________
14. ______________________
15. ______________________
16. ______________________
17. ______________________
18. ______________________
19. ______________________
20. ______________________
21. ______________________
22. ______________________
23. ______________________
24. ______________________